Growing Pains

Happy 1995 Birthday
Carol —
Enjoy this book as
you dream of
digging in the dirt!
Love
Willie

Also by Patricia Thorpe

Everlastings: The Complete Book of Dried Flowers (1986)

The American Weekend Garden (1988)

America's Cottage Gardens (1990)

ILLUSTRATIONS BY *Judy Clifford*

Growing

PATRICIA THORPE

Pains

....

TIME AND

CHANGE

IN THE GARDEN

A Harvest Book
Harcourt Brace & Company
San Diego   New York   London

Requests for permission to make copies of any part of the work
should be mailed to: Permissions Department,
Harcourt Brace & Company, 6277 Sea Harbor Drive,
Orlando, Florida 32887-6777.

Library of Congress Cataloging-in-Publication Data
Thorpe, Patricia.
    Growing pains: time and change in the garden/Patricia Thorpe:
illustrations by Judy Clifford. — 1st ed.
        p.   cm.
    Includes index.
    ISBN 0-15-600201-9
    1. Gardening. 2. Gardening — United States. 3. Landscape
gardening. 4. Landscape gardening — United States.   I. Title.
SB453.T486   1994
635.9—dc20   93-42605

Designed by Trina Stahl
Printed in the United States of America
First Harvest edition 1995
A B C D E

For Harry, who has survived these growing pains and many others

Contents

· ·

Contents

1

Discovering

the Midlife Crisis

in Your Garden

....

It TOOK MOST of us forty or fifty years to reach a midlife crisis— how could our gardens achieve it in less than a decade? But how else can we describe the state of the landscapes we see before us? Bushes are too big or too close together; trees have sprung up to cut off our views and shade our roses; our once-mixed perennial borders now seem to contain only three species, all of them yellow. We have paths that no one will take; patios no one will sit on; places to go and no way to get to them. We have surrounded ourselves with colors of unspeakable horror; we have gone out of our way to cultivate species of unredeemed mediocrity or suspicious personal habits.

The symptoms are all too familiar, especially to anyone who came through the seventies reading Gail Sheehy: the sense of indecision or stagnation; the lack of direction; the reluctance to adjust to inevitable physical changes; too much of some things and not enough of others; a tendency to fall into familiar patterns instead of seeking new inspiration. There is the disconcerting sense that the garden, something we once thought of as our creation, is evolving in unexpected ways, growing beyond some of our aspirations while coming up woefully short with respect to others.

Some of us respond to these changes with denial. We refuse to admit that the cryptomeria has cut off access to the mailbox; we continue to force our way through paths that were once a little too narrow and are now impassible to anyone without a machete. Others do not stop to analyze the situation but simply announce that they are tearing the whole thing out and starting over. A few may declare that they are giving up completely and moving to an apartment. Even if our responses are less extreme, we may notice definite changes in our gardens before they reach the end of their first decade. For some gardens it will be a seven-year itch. Others may be faster or slower to mature to this dangerous stage. This, to use Gail Sheehy's term, is the first "predictable crisis" of the garden's life.

Any garden, even a vegetable plot, involves a great many life cycles. We see the manic life span of the radish or mustard cress, from seed to seed in a matter of weeks, compared to the barely perceptible growth of the bristlecone pine, which may live on for a thousand years after we plant it. But in spite of this enormous variety, and in spite of the many kinds of gardens and the many kinds of people who make them, there are some easily recognizable stages of development that are common to all. There are the early years when the trees are spindly and still have their labels fluttering in the wind—those bygone days when the mulch spread in thick, brown, weedless layers around knee-high conifers and you could still remember the names of everything. Then there are the years of encouragement, after the plants start to grow but before the deer discover their presence—the short span during which perennials actually come back every year and botrytis doesn't come back with them. This is frequently a period of happy, headlong over-expansion when, buoyed by living evidence of our early success, we plunge heavily into roses or obscure evergreens and decide that a single hundred-foot-long perennial border is hardly enough. Then we enter the years of crisis, when the growth we so long awaited arrives all at once and the solitary problems we have tried to ignore suddenly seem overwhelming. This crisis is not merely a result of the precise stage of the garden, but of the combination of garden problems that have accumulated over time with the realization, which seems to be growing as quickly as kudzu, that there really is a lot we don't know about gardening.

A garden seven to ten years old clearly is nowhere near its midlife. When we think of the Villa Lante, still thriving in Viterbo four hundred years after its creation, ten years seems barely adolescent. In fact, if we want to explore another series of self-help clichés, there are similarities between our garden's state and that of adolescent angst, and if we are experiencing that traumatic period with our children we may be inclined to describe our garden in those terms. But most of us who have gardened a decade or more are a lot closer to middle age than to adolescence and we are more likely to see in our gardens' malaise many of the symptoms of our own somewhat reluctant transition to a new stage of life.

Even in our youth-obsessed culture we realize that a young garden has a long way to go before it reaches the beauties of maturity. We idolize the gardens of ages past and long for centuries-old oaks and boxwood twenty feet high. Yet we are unprepared for the awkward phases that will fill the decades between now and then. Even while we acknowledge that growth is the essence of the garden, we are afraid to face some of the changes that growth will bring. Many of us have a similar blind spot with respect to the growth of our children. We would be hysterical if each trip to the pediatrician did not document extra pounds and more inches, but we cannot admit that this growth leads inevitably to Rollerblades, rock music, purple hair, pierced ears, and possibly tattoos. We want our gardens to grow, but we also want them to stay the way we planted them. We want the shrubs to maintain the neat sizes and shapes they had in the nursery; we want the conifers to remain evergreen geometrical solids. We may admire, in the abstract, the abundant multiplicity of nature, but we might not be prepared to see it unleashed in our own backyards.

Some Historic Background for a Climate of Crisis

ALL GARDENERS FACE certain crisis stages as their gardens mature and as their understanding of gardening grows along with their plants. There are problems that we all face toward the end of our first ten years of gardening, and problems some of us may face forty years from now. Some of these have confronted gardeners from the time of the first hoe, but there are others that are specific to Americans who began to garden in the last twenty years.

Although the United States has had a few distinct periods during which elaborate gardens were made, gardening is not a significant part of American culture. It may be listed as our most popular leisure pursuit, but gardening is a quiet and individual pastime; it does not make headlines or proselytize. In the past, the people who grew up gardening tended to pursue it while the rest of the population simply admired or ignored the outcome.

The sixties and seventies saw a gradual increase in gardening among people who had never done it before. This was partly the result of the back-to-nature urges of the decades' counterculture: communes lived off the land

and flower children discovered the wonders of nature and fresh vegetables. But a more mainstream movement was developing at the same time as an increasing number of suburban homeowners became bored with the low-maintenance landscape. The lawn-and-foundation-planting formula had taken hold of hundreds of housing developments back in the thirties, and in the postwar period this pattern was reinforced by the rapid decline in the availability of professional gardeners. America had never had a strong tradition of highly skilled, well-trained gardeners, but before the war people could at least get someone to "see to things"—digging beds, planting trees, edging walks, staking up, cutting down. Increased education and improved employment opportunities after the war brought an end to that level of labor, and American homeowners were left to manage as best they could. What most of them decided they could manage was half an acre of lawn and some evergreens under the windows.

By the mid-sixties a lot of suburban settlers were ready for a change. The low-maintenance landscape did not turn out to be so care-free after all, and some homeowners decided that if they had to rake and mow and weed the pachysandra, they might as well put in a little extra effort and have more to show for it. The California doctrine of outdoor living was gaining converts, even in areas where the climate allowed outdoor living only one month of the year. Patios and pool decks proliferated, along with the need to shield them and shade them and blend them into the landscape. Another California phenomenon, the garden center, started selling plants where people spent most of their time—along the highways. Container growing revolutionized the marketing of plants by making a wide variety of material easy to transplant and easy to transport to virtually every part of the country. No longer was it necessary to grow your own from seed or start with barely visible bare-root sticks. No longer were plants raised and sold by cautious, knowledgeable, and intimidating local growers. Azaleas in full flower from South Carolina could be shipped to Vermont in a few days, where they would meet almost certain death at the hands of innocent enthusiasts who didn't know the meaning of hardiness.

Through the seventies, gardening continued to grow steadily in popularity. Sturdy flowering plants were being marketed that could lure timid homeowners away from the monotony of evergreens: day lilies, stunning varieties of azaleas, compact ornamental trees, foolproof impatiens. This was hardly explosive expansion, but it was a great leap forward after several decades of bluegrass and capitata yews. Garden clubs became less concerned with social status and more active in environmental concerns and public education. Botanical gardens and arboretums began making more active attempts to involve people in courses and volunteer programs. Changing culinary trends had their impact as herbs became fashionable and outré vegetables commonplace. It was exciting to find that horticulture was heading toward the mainstream. All this was nothing, however, to what happened in the eighties.

In the eighties, gardening became trendy. Along with fine food and fancy decorating, gardening became the window dressing of the good life. And as entertaining in the eighties meant not just a good meal but an elaborate event, so gardening became more than just growing your own arugula. People wanted perennial borders and teakwood benches, laburnum allées and boxwood parterres. Among the newly wealthy, there was a brief reenactment of the Golden Age as formal landscapes were created to accessorize extravagant houses. Hot garden designers became as sought after as top caterers or "in" decorators. Professional gardeners were no longer septuagenarian handymen with battered trucks and uncertain English, but elegant individuals with accents from Wellesley or Oxford and BMWs that seemed perfectly at home in an East Hampton driveway.

That was the conspicuous high end of garden making. But the vast majority of converts to horticulture were not despoilers of savings-and-loan institutions, nor did they need to be. Gardening has usually been a low-budget entertainment, and if the budgets were somewhat higher in the eighties than they had been in decades, they were still a great deal less than what many people were spending on upholstering. The new gardeners were different from previous gardening generations in America. They were younger and better educated and financially more secure. Many were Anglophiles. They were well-read in garden literature and enamored of the classic garden traditions. They were ambitious for their gardens. And they were wonderfully ignorant about most of the basics of horticulture.

It is never hard to start a garden, even if you know nothing about plants.

Now, to make it easier still, there were garden designers who would lay out flower borders and give in to extravagant fantasies like rose-covered pergolas. There were mail-order outlets offering color-coordinated perennial collections and tapestry hedges by the yard, not to mention arbors, fountains, follies, and fragments of gothic ruins. The last twenty years had brought an abundance of beautiful books to the shelves, most of them concerned with getting people started. Of course there was the considerable labor of digging all those holes, but once you had the plants in the ground you were well on your way. With enough Lutyens benches scattered around the landscape, the whole place almost looked like, well, if not a vision of paradise, at least the cover of a Smith & Hawken catalog. There seemed no reason to believe that gardening would be any more difficult than cooking or decorating: You bought the right book, you acquired the right ingredients, followed a formula that looked good on the page, and put everything together. Suddenly you had a garden.

But unlike a gourmet meal, a garden exists over time—not just weeks or months, but many years. Unlike a living room, it is growing and changing. What you see is not at all what you are going to get ten years from now. Setting out the plants is the barest beginning of our work and the only moment we can completely control. Once the plants are in the ground, they are launched on their independent lives. We can observe them and enjoy them; we can slowly get to know them. We can mourn them when they fail to survive. We can only try to control them and change them. We learn to garden, not from books and photographs, but from the gradual accumulation of detail about the lives of the plants and the development of the garden as we experience it. And during this slow process of education, our gardens have been turning into jungles around us.

So Many Gardeners; So Little Help

D URING A MERICA'S LAST great gardening boom, from the turn of the century through the thirties, there were also large numbers of enthusiastic and ignorant individuals who plunged into horticulture. Many of them, like the new gardeners of the eighties, had high ambitions and heavy wallets.

Unlike today's gardeners, they had help, and lots of it. Top gardeners from the British Isles were coaxed away from their native land. Craftsmen from all over the world were among the waves of immigrants, providing stone-masons, woodworkers, pathlayers, and earthmovers without limit. America still had a large agricultural society, so even if you were not among the richest of the *nouveaux riches,* you could still find someone locally who knew how to till the soil, apply manure, prune the fruit trees, and set out beds of annuals.

The circumstances for today's gardeners are entirely different. Most of us are thankful if we can get someone to mow the lawn without causing significant bodily harm to themselves or to those we love. Anything more demanding horticulturally is definitely in the realm of do-it-yourself. (The incompetent hired gardener was a stock comic figure in the literature of the Golden Age. I suspect most of us read those passages today with longing. The autocratic author of *Elizabeth and Her German Garden* toys with her amateur garden schemes and fires the various half-wits who stand in her way; I find myself crying out, "I'll take him! I'll take him!") Labor-saving technology can help us to some extent by providing small mobile tractors, chain saws, Weed Eaters, leaf blowers, and watering systems, but having a chain saw does not ensure that you know what and when to cut, and it is hard to make the best use of a Weed Eater if you're still not sure what is a weed and what isn't.

During the last twenty years in America, more people embarked on more ambitious garden making with less information and less help than at any time in the last two centuries. The tidal wave of books published during this time attempted to address the information gap, but most of them either described the most basic planting procedures and problems or detailed the many species of esoteric saxifrages or asarum we might someday aspire to grow. We were shown a great many brand-new gardens and many gardens generations old. The first stages of gardening have been written up as thoroughly as the first months of a baby's life, and for exactly the same reasons. Although babies are individuals, all new parents face nearly the same changes and discoveries. As the babies mature, their unique combinations of characteristics become more evident and their care becomes harder to generalize.

Recent gardening literature gives us the sense that once we have staked out our paths and double dug our first border, there is little more to do than scour the catalogs for more and more obscure plants each year. We don't see glossy photographs of how the rose beds look after the first winter of subzero temperatures. We are not shown what a perennial border looks like if you don't quite get around to weeding it for a month. We delight in pictures of exquisite plant combinations we might someday hope to imitate, but aren't told that *Paeonia mlokosewitschii* stays in bloom for about three days, assuming it doesn't rain or get too hot.

Starting a garden is a little like starting a love affair. You can coast for quite a while on all the early excitement and enthusiasm. And because of the forgiving nature of plants, the early romance stage may persist for somewhat longer than it does between two lovers. In spite of our ignorance, plants live and grow and even bloom. It may take us a while to discover that this early success is one of the subtle forms of tyranny a garden can exercise, a horticultural version of passive aggression. Plants live, and we may live to regret it. How pleased we were when that frail Norway maple in front of the picture window showed signs of survival. We are a little less pleased now that a dark pall of shade covers what remains of the front lawn and sunlight penetrates the living room only after several tons of leaves have fallen in October. The perfect little herb garden we started, as finely arranged as the corner of a medieval tapestry for the first year, has turned into a battleground for applemint and *Artemisia* "Silver King" by its third season. The creeping juniper that would not condescend to cover the steep bank you had in mind has no scruples about creeping across the driveway and occupying the parking area. One unbearable aspect of our gardens' success is the way their growth inexorably magnifies all our youthful mistakes. Most of us can now look back with something like nostalgic fondness upon the personal peccadillos of our pasts; we might not feel that way if they were displayed on a billboard. But that is what the landscape does to our early gardening misadventures—it magnifies them, sets them in lights, lets all the world know that in a moment of weakness we flirted with a neon azalea, once thought a multiflora rose hedge was just what we needed, briefly believed aegopodium might make a pretty ground cover. It is unnecessary to say that these mistakes are always our most enduring plantings.

With such successes one hardly needs failures, but of course we have failures as well. When we start out gardening, we are prepared for failures to some degree, just as we are prepared for the separation of our first hollandaise and the fall of our first soufflé. But our gardening disasters are more enigmatic than that. Plants thrive for years and then die before our eyes. A maple that stood for generations comes crashing down without warning. A magnolia that was covered with blossoms last year has three this spring. We unexpectedly discover that the new foliage of our favorite pine tree is a mass of naked green worms. And why do they call these things perennials if they keep dying? All the experience we have gained in the last decade seems to make no difference. In fact, we seem to be killing off more plants than ever.

All gardens, even those of experienced horticulturists, need serious reassessment and replanting every seven to ten years. The knowledgeable plantsman accepts this as a matter of course; the beginner discovers this in the course of a nervous breakdown. This is why the first predictable crisis in our gardens is such a watershed. A certain percentage of new gardeners decides at this point that gardening is too hard or too boring, that it is impossible to get help, that a tennis court would make better use of all that outdoor space, that starting over is the only solution and that it is too late to start over. These feelings are similar to those that characterize a personal midlife crisis—feelings that can result in such drastic life changes as divorce or moving to California. In the garden crisis, as in the personal one, it is important to realize that this is a clearly defined period all gardens must survive before they move on to greater maturity and real beauty. Yes, this garden can be saved. You will have to rip some things up, but not everything. Some of your early design concepts will have to be abandoned, but much can be salvaged. There is abundant plant material that can be better employed now that you understand how it behaves. There are plants you once killed that you can now grow. Whether you realize it yet or not, you have learned a great deal about your climate and growing conditions over the past ten years—now you can start using that knowledge to make your gardening easier, or if not easier, at least more rewarding. You now know a great deal more about the kind of garden you want to create. Once you clear out some of the wreckage, you can go on to make that garden.

Reassessing Your Relationships

ANY GOOD MIDLIFE crisis forces us to examine our relationships with those nearest and dearest. No, you don't have to start accusing your mother or railing at your spouse; instead, start asking yourself how you feel about different parts of your garden. One consequence of the high ambitions of eighties gardening was that people acquired a lot of garden before they knew what to do with it. Rose gardens were planted by beginners who had never experienced a rose outside of a florist's bouquet. Perennial borders were ordered by individuals who were not quite sure just what a perennial was. Herb gardens were "in," so we acquired six flavors of thyme. We all received a Meadow-in-a-Can for Christmas one year, so a meadow garden went on the agenda. The whole gamut may have been in the ground before we had any idea what was needed to keep each plant alive—before we realized that the demands of one are different from those of another. After ten years, parts of the garden may have fallen victim to climate, pests, disease, and our own inexperience; others might simply have been reclaimed by the landscape. Time makes clear to us which parts of the garden can survive; it is up to us to determine which we really like, which we never visit, which work with our schedule and our home life—the demands of the resident soccer players vs. the rights of the resident delphinium grower.

Some kinds of gardens are easier to control than others, and we seldom know that when we start out. Different gardens have different dynamics. For a vegetable garden or a bed of annuals, the cycle of growth and change extends over one season only. No matter if it is a success or a failure, its life span is finished at the first frost. Although there is still plenty of room for catastrophe, the gardener has maximum control over her material if she faces a clean slate every spring. The low-maintenance landscape is a similarly low-risk situation. The gardener uses a limited range of material with clearly defined habits of growth. If you follow the rules—mow the lawn every week, clip the yews once or twice a year—the plants will behave themselves, and you will still be in charge.

A formal rose garden demands a great deal more work than a patch of pachysandra, but it is not difficult to control. If you follow the formulas you can succeed. It is not the kind of garden that is inclined to take off in an unexpected direction, unless you don't have a climate or soil that agrees with roses (in which case the direction will be abruptly downhill). But you might not like covering the landscape with chemical clouds every ten days, and you might find that although it is rewarding to have an armful of roses, you long for some variety and change throughout the season. Sprawling informal beds of many kinds of perennials may appear much more nonchalant than a rose bed, but they could require just as much effort with more unpredictable results because you are trying to understand the needs of many different kinds of plants, and you are trying to meet all those needs in one place. A meadow garden looks like a carefree way to enjoy flowers, but as you may have discovered with your Meadow-in-a-Can experiment, your collection of wildflowers will soon consist of ragweed and burdocks if you don't give it the same attention required of a traditional bed of annuals. A naturalistic effect can be as hard to maintain as a rigidly formal scheme of clipped hedges and perfect turf, depending on the kind of work you like to do and the kind of help you can get. You might have thought a rock garden would be easy—little plants, small place, less work, right? But many of those tiny plants make big demands on our time and attention. Although the space they take up is small, every aspect of the environment has to be controlled to keep the plants alive—just one slug could spell disaster on that scale. If control is important to you, you may have to give up on areas of the landscape that cannot be kept in order. If your garden style tends toward confusion, you had better not consider projects like a vegetable plot, which are hopeless without some organizing principle.

Impossible Dreams

I T ' S   N O T   T O O hard to give up the roses or the vegetables, once you admit that they don't work for you. It may be far more difficult to surrender your early ideas of what a garden ought to be. Young gardens created by new gardeners can be pretty, but generally they have very little to say. Most gardeners just starting out have a very conventional notion of what a garden is; they want a garden that looks like a photograph in a book or on a calendar. (This should hardly surprise us, when we consider how many years we might have wasted trying to mold ourselves to fit conventional and unrealistic ideals of beauty or success.) If you work at it hard enough, for one or two seasons you can manage to achieve the kind of picture-perfect triumph to be found in a flower-show display. But this is not the kind of garden that can move us or inspire us or interest us for very long, quite aside from the impossible amount of work involved. A midlife crisis erupts when you discover that you can no longer sustain the illusion that you have re-created Giverney on a half acre in central Kansas, or when you admit that Sissinghurst might be beyond you. For a decade your climate and landscape have tried to convince you that this fantasy was not going to work. There are wonderful gardens to be made in central Kansas, but Giverney is not one of them.

Toward the end of the first decade of gardening you are poised between the garden of your fantasies and your slowly accumulating knowledge of what you may actually achieve someday. This is very similar to the stage of life in which you realize that you will never be as rich, as powerful, as clever, as seductive, as young as the images with which the world surrounds you. The conditions of your climate remind you that you are probably not living in Kent or the south of France. You have the further specifics of your soil, probably as far from being "good garden soil" as you are from being a Vogue model. You have the unique details of your landscape, which can vary even among neighbors in one subdivision. All these "givens" of a property are the limitations against which you struggle, at first, in your need to make a garden like those of everyone else. One of the fascinations of the Golden Age gardens is the fact that the need to imitate European culture triumphed,

at least in the short run, over all these factors of the American continent, as well as over common sense and good taste. These were gardens that labored against great odds to make Americans believe that Vignola had once wandered the streets of Tulsa, or that the Petit Trianon had originally been built in Rhode Island. These were gardens that could not give up their illusions. Few of them survive to any extent today, and the few that do are more ludicrous than beautiful—their pathetic urge to be anything other than themselves is painfully apparent.

Even at the heights of eighties extravagance, no one was prepared to go quite as far as the follies of the Golden Age. But garden designers in Dallas still get clients who ask them to create "something English"; in Los Angeles, people are still trying to grow seven-foot-tall delphiniums in the midst of drought. (In Southern California it would make more sense to imitate the Villa Lante than to cultivate ten acres of lawn, and some of the more successful Golden Age gardens did just that.) If you are spending more time sighing over pictures of Sissinghurst than you are hauling compost or digging out polygonums, you are still held in thrall by someone else's idea of a garden.

This is the time to determine what works and what doesn't; this is the time to dig up and cut back and throw out and move around. Some of this will be depressing at first, but despair will be followed by excitement as the garden takes on a new life. The garden that survives its growing pains may appear more eccentric as it ventures further from the familiar clichés of planting. It is a garden that is on its way toward expressing a unique vision of the landscape, a vision shaped by experience and personal opinion and knowledge of the natural world.

Some new gardeners gave up during the last ten years, and some may not survive the crisis we now face. But in spite of our early misadventures, many of us are beginning to understand what gardening is about. It is no longer the end result that is all important—a crucial realization, since the result we see before us now might be distinctly discouraging. It is the long-term process of making a garden that we must love if we are to persist; it is the lifelong project of watching things grow or not grow and trying to understand why or why not. It is an eternity of studying the relationships among insects and plants, between plants and weather, between weather and landscape, between nature and ourselves.

New Adventures, New Disasters

THIS IS AN exciting time to be gardening; it is also challenging. Although many of the problems faced by new gardeners today are those that have faced garden makers forever, there are some specific difficulties. For example, there is a bewildering abundance of plants available. Ill-placed nostalgia prompts some of us to bemoan the gardens of long ago and the flowers now lost to commerce, but many of those old-fashioned flowers are available again. Besides the favorites of yesteryear, there are many, many new plants coming on the market. Yes, there are yet more varieties of petunias or marigolds that we don't need. But along with them are new species from China and Japan; more and more of our native plants are being brought into cultivation; and unheard-of treasures just being discovered in South America are slowly making their way to propagation ranges, then on to the backyards of America.

This plethora of new material brings with it confusion as well as excitement. New plants are not tested like new drugs or food before they reach the retail market. Major seed and plant dealers may field-test new species before offering them, but they seldom study the material in a wide variety of climates through a decade or more of growth. There is vast uncertainty about how any plant will respond to a new growing situation, even plants that have been in cultivation for centuries. How much more unpredictable is the performance of a plant newly arrived from the lowlands of China or the mountains of New Zealand? Such plants once remained within circles of experts, who experimented with them for many years before sending them on to the general public. Today we can buy iris species from China that were unknown even five years ago in this country. This is thrilling for many of us, but the uncertainty of the unknown may be discouraging to gardeners who prefer that their plants survive. One reason the recent gardening boom has been so exciting is because many of the new gardeners were ambitious about what they wanted to do and adventurous about what they wanted to grow. Some of those new gardeners had no idea how adventurous they were—they may not have known that gentians can be touchy about lime, or that primulas are resentful of high temperatures, or that cytisus doesn't like wind. So it is hardly surprising that some of them are now asking themselves what went wrong. We all fail with certain plants, and not only the difficult ones—I have a long history of disaster with dahlias and African marigolds. One of the delights and frustrations of gardening is that there will always be new beauties that elude our best efforts to grow them, and there will always be a few impossibilities that suddenly, after years of failure, decide to thrive.

True Confessions

I CANNOT SAY that I have solved all the problems of the midlife crisis; I merely had the advantage of experiencing them somewhat earlier than many of today's gardeners. And writing about these problems often goaded me into tackling my more egregious failures and trying to set them right. But I have also had the benefit of traveling around the United States and Canada, meeting hundreds of gardeners—both amateur and professional—seeing their remarkable successes, and hearing about their failures.

Although some of our midlife problems may go back to basic mistakes in our early planting procedures, I have tried to avoid restating the usual beginner formulas and instead concentrated on the problems and solutions to be found in a garden that has been growing for several years. Recognizing that there are special problems to be faced in the first decade is the important first step. After working our way through the major manifestations of the crisis, I want to suggest ways in which the garden can expand during its next stage of growth. I also want to raise some of the environmental issues that gardeners should consider, issues of which we were hardly aware when we started out, but which become more and more pressing each day.

Growing up with gardening does not keep you from making stupid mistakes: I am an excellent case in point. You can be sure that many of the disasters detailed here have happened to me. Growing up in one climate and landscape, with one set of plants, does not prepare you for the gardens of your future. And a long childhood spent pinching back pansies or pulling up purslane did not keep me from having my own highly unrealistic illusions about what could be done in a rocky pasture in upstate New York. But growing up in a garden does prepare you for several important realizations: that disasters are just one part of the fabric of the garden; that growth and change are essential and desirable even if they drive you crazy; that the garden requires a commitment of attention over a period of time even longer than that required to raise a child—with some of the same rewards.

We survived the food fads of the eighties and no longer have to endure pomegranate vinaigrette and honey mustard drizzled over every dish. But even in this period of welcome culinary simplicity, we can see how American cuisine as a whole benefited enormously from the trendiness of the last decade. Fresh herbs like basil and marjoram are available year-round; unheard-of vegetables and fruit like atamoyas or salsify or black chanterelles can be bought in corner grocery stores; and bread, real bread, is on the streets.

In the same way, we can be grateful for some of the changes the gardening fads of the eighties have brought. We have abundant new plants and a network of regional growers who are getting innovative material out to gardeners. We have new technology for dealing with environmental problems like watering, erosion, and pest control. We have a new generation of garden designers who are sensitive to ecological issues and who are eager to work with a more innovative palette of plants. We have a wonderful new organization, the Garden Conservancy, which is working to preserve our American garden heritage and to make it known to today's gardeners. Best of all, we have more people gardening, reading about gardening, thinking about gardening, talking about gardening. Gradually the trendiness will die away: people will no longer spend two hundred dollars for the perfect rose pruners or the right pair of gloves, and we will be left with more and better American gardening. We may not be able to maintain our early fantasies of garden making. We may have to give up on a two-hundred-foot-long perennial border or a rose-covered pergola that doesn't quite make it through the North Dakota winter, but there will be other illusions to replace them. There will be future frustrations and unexpected catastrophes. There will also be delights we could hardly have imagined. But only if we keep on gardening.

2

Too Much

....

$\mathcal{W}e$ TRAVELED LIGHT in the early part of our lives—now suddenly we feel overwhelmed by possessions. Too many suit jackets that are just a little tight across the shoulders or skirts we may be able to wear again once we start exercise class. Too many *Scientific American*s we may someday go back and read; too many unopened cartons of books from that club we keep meaning to quit. We have gone from being people who entertained on cushions on the floor to people who are wondering what to do with that extra dining-room table. We never had two toothbrushes; now we have two houses.

Not everyone has this problem to the same degree, but to some extent accumulation is an unfailing result of time. Some of us confine the excess to the waistline, others to the garage, but most of us reach a point where we feel we have too much stuff.

Looking at the landscape, we can see the same problem. What was once wide open space has become crowded with plants. All those supposedly slow-growing shrubs, barely visible for years unless the lawn was cut, have sprung up to cover windows and press against paths. The trees that were set out to frame the view are now obscuring it. The carefully balanced perennial border has turned into a battleground between two gigantic species you never liked in the first place. It can happen in five years, it is bound to happen in ten—suddenly, in the garden, we have too much stuff.

We all make the same mistakes when we start out, and, if it makes us feel any better, professional landscape contractors do, too. Faced with the bare outline of a new house on an empty lot, the urge to shove in lots of greenery is irresistible. Fill that foundation; call in the ground covers; no plant is too large or too close for comfort. Unscrupulous landscapers prey on our insecurity by providing several times the material we need, and even reputable designers give in to the complaints of customers who "don't want it to look skimpy." Unless we have had a great deal of experience with plants, we simply cannot envision how big a tree will grow, and how quickly. We also don't keep track of the vastly different rates at which plants develop, although the information is in many books and most catalogs. When two shrubs started out in the same two-gallon containers, how could we imagine that the Exbury azalea would grow a mere three inches in five years while the mock orange at its side shot up to six feet?

This is not merely a common problem—it is an almost universal one. It is just as common not to realize that the problem exists. We get used to ducking branches that block the path, accustomed to easing the car through the tunnel of a driveway. We forget that windows used to let in light, not just tendrils of wisteria. If you have bought someone else's middle-aged garden, it is easier to see the confusion of overplanting; if you planted all those things yourself, you may not have noticed how they crept up around you. Who would have thought success could be such a problem?

Much of our plant accumulation begins right around the house. If you built or bought a new house, the bare foundation seemed to demand immediate attention. If you acquired an older home, you probably set about clearing out the plant accumulations of the previous owner, but that may not have prevented you from making the same misjudgments. Most new gardeners simply replace the mistakes of the last generation with shrubs that will be equally overgrown in a few years. Some of this activity is guided by plant trendiness—the clipped geometrical shapes of yew and arborvitae, all the rage of the postwar period, are being ousted for dwarf conifers; magenta azaleas are replaced by Korean lilacs and *Rhododendron yakusimanum*. Although many of these plants are described as dwarf, that doesn't mean they are not going to grow, and it is a bold landscape contractor who will actually set them out eight or ten feet apart when the homeowner wants his foundation covered and wants it covered *now*.

We can be misled into overplanting in a number of ways. The bare look of a new house seems to demand greenery—we long to apply it the way architects do in their imaginative mock-ups, with sweeps of lush growth healing the scars left by construction. And there is no doubt that heavy planting can give a new house the look of being a part of the landscape, at least until it looks as if the house was devoured by the landscape. But new

home builders are not alone in their desire for an immediate effect. We have all become accustomed to the concept of instant gratification, and newcomers to gardening often see no reason why decorating a landscape should be any different from decorating a living room. You buy what you want and put it where you want it and that is that. Except for one crucial difference: In your living room, buying and placing the furnishings is the end of decorating, while in gardening it is just the beginning of an independent life for your plants. More knowledgeable gardeners can be led astray by too much enthusiasm: We just fall in love with plants, and want to live with as many as possible. We flirt with roses; we are seduced by heathers; we surround ourselves with a harem of dwarf conifers of startling diversity. After a few years of somewhat promiscuous affection, we may begin to understand the advantages of monogamy.

There are many plants on the market today that have been developed specifically for the smaller garden. There are dwarf conifers that would seem to make ideal foundation plants, and slow-growing specimens intended for limited space. But there is a common misconception about so-called dwarf plants. Dwarf is a relative rather than an absolute term. A dwarf spruce may not grow to eighty feet but it can still reach ten—and more quickly than you thought possible. Many dwarfs are not really dwarf at all, but simply slow-growing in the early years of development. They may appear as inanimate as plastic plants for the first ten years, then suddenly shoot up to double their size in a season. Height is not the only factor. My bird's nest spruce, fifteen years old, is still under three feet in height, but even after being moved twice it is the circumference of a table for six. To add to the confusion, there are abundant cultivated varieties of the most popular shrubs, and they can differ widely in size and rate of growth. A mugho pine is not just a mugho pine. If it is *Pinus mugo* "Paul's Dwarf," it might grow an inch a year, while *Pinus mugo* "Big Tuna" could easily leap above four feet in ten years. (I have a standard dwarf mugho, described in a reference book before me as always being under six feet, and rarely over four feet except in prime conditions. This one is certainly not in prime conditions, since it sits in soggy clay, but it is quite a bit over five feet high now, and has spent less than twenty years in my garden.) So we should be aware that, although there are smaller plants available, we still can manage to buy too many of them, and even the ones that are small and slow can be in the wrong place after ten years.

Having too much can be a functional problem: you can no longer see through the *Magnolia grandiflora* in front of the window; the junipers edging the steps have now edged out all human traffic. It can be a horticultural problem: the shrubs in the mixed border have grown so closely into one another that you couldn't tell one from the next even if they bloomed, which they don't. It can be a design problem: the once-clear outline of the garden has become confused, the movement through it hesitant as paths dwindle and branches threaten. It can be an aesthetic problem: you have managed to put together a selection of plants that simply look awful together. Regardless of how it happened and why, we have to face this happy excess and figure out what to do about it.

Cutting Back or Cutting Down

WHEN IT HAPPENS in your house you can have a garage sale or call the Salvation Army, but what do you do when you find that your adorable chamaecyparis has taken over your doorstep? When you first started to garden, you were enormously grateful when something happened to live— it seemed like a miracle. How can you possibly betray a staunch survivor from those early days by cutting it down? You probably tried to forestall the inevitable by what you thought of as judicious pruning. This can sometimes give you a little more leeway, but many plants will just end up looking awkward, like a child wearing clothes he outgrew a year ago. Eager shoots sprout up from unexpected places, trying to elude the shears. Even an adept and tactful pruner can only do so much. Besides, this creates a terrible drain on our gardening time. One variety of gardener likes nothing better than to pass the day carving evergreens into chess figures and animals, but most of us would rather not be chained to the secateurs. Constant vigilance is the price of topiary.

If you don't want to cut them down, and you are sick of cutting them back, you can try to deal with your overabundance of plants by moving them. It isn't always easy, and it isn't always successful. When moving isn't successful you may decide it would have been easier to cut down your problems in the first place. Too many gardeners are intimidated by the look of permanence a plant acquires after being in one place for a while. This illusion reinforces our inclination to live with our problems rather than to do something about them. Moving plants, even big, well-established plants, is an integral part of life in a maturing garden, and the sooner we get started the better.

Moving Out

Recognizing that you have too much is a big first step. Now you have to begin sorting it out. You probably have enough good-sized shrubs in against your house to landscape another garden. One landscape designer told me: "I could have a business making gardens out of overcrowded foundations—I wouldn't even need a nursery." If much of your original planting was done by someone else, you may not have had a lot of experience moving large plants. Even if you did it yourself, popping carefully pruned shrubs out of their neat plastic containers seems simple compared with the prospect of yanking up something that has been in the ground for several years. It is rather like cleaning out the garage—the job is much worse when you're thinking about it ahead of time. Once you have the first plants out, it won't seem quite so bad.

There is no harm in playing favorites. It is more than likely that your early indiscriminate buying brought some fairly dull bushes into your life. It is also inevitable that these are the ones that are growing best, but they may be crowding out plants you really like, so these should be the first to go. Besides, they will be good practice for your plant-moving techniques. Of course, you don't have to try to salvage them; but I have found that most gardeners, particularly at this juncture of their lives, are reluctant to be sufficiently ruthless (give them another twenty years and they are happy to cut down anything in sight). Most of us feel responsibility for plants we don't even like.

With any luck, there should be some plants that never did well in the first place. We will talk more about that in the next chapter, but for now, stragglers and malingerers should be disposed of without a backward glance. Then turn to the opposite. It may seem unfair to eliminate anything that has been wildly successful, but those are probably the shrubs that are leaning on others, crowding out better-behaved members of the group. These are the shrubs you find yourself cutting back three or four times a year to keep them within bounds. They are likely to grow with equal eagerness somewhere else, somewhere they can grow at their own rate and reach their natural proportions. The plants you want to keep around foundations or close to paths and drives should be low growing and slow growing.

This is your chance to give more coherence to some of your shrub plantings. Now that you have lived with these plants for years, you must have a better idea of what looks good with what than you did when you first put them in. Wouldn't this be a good time to move the yellow- and gold-toned azaleas away from the magenta ones that bloom at the same time? Wouldn't the white potentilla, "Abbotswood," look better in front of some dark conifers, instead of half-buried under the lilacs? How about that bed that resembles a Whitman sampler—of the dozen or so genera represented, why not take out ten? Please keep in mind that shifting things around is secondary to the major goal of clearing out.

Rhododendrons and azaleas are among the easiest shrubs to move because of their shallow root systems. If they have turned out to blossom in colors you could do without, they might find happy homes among your neighbors, who might even come and dig them up for you. Roses are easier to move than you would expect, once you get past the thorns. Cut them back hard in late winter and dig as soon as the ground begins to thaw. The best time to dig most flowering shrubs is after they bloom, but they can be moved anytime from late winter on if you don't mind sacrificing one season of flowers. Your timing may depend on your ability to be around to water them and keep them shaded after the move. Conifers can be risky, but even using fairly primitive methods we have had remarkable success shifting them around in our garden.

Ideally, you can prepare for moving ahead of time by top pruning and root pruning the shrub in the summer and again in the fall, then moving the plant early the following spring. But let's face it: few of us have that kind of foresight. I usually find that the argument for root pruning is a way of putting off for yet another season something that should have been done years ago. Even without advance root pruning you will probably have a reasonable rate of success. After you have moved a few large specimens, you may be happier with the thought of cutting things down.

There are no big secrets to success in moving plants—like most gardening, it requires little more than basic common sense. The top of the plant should be pruned back, then tied in or wrapped as close as possible around the trunk. The root ball should have approximately the same circumference as the spread of the top of the plant. Spade in a circle around the root ball to sever roots, then dig a trench about a foot wide, using the first circle as the inside edge. After you have removed the soil from the trench, cut down at roughly a forty-five-degree angle toward the center of the ball, working all around the plant. When you have cut away the roots, slide plastic or burlap under and around the ball, and tie it at the top of the roots. Now you are ready to move.

It is easy to describe the idealized moving operation, but clearly in practice there will be some setbacks. For one thing, if you had enough space to dig a trench a foot wide around this particular plant, you probably wouldn't need to move it. You will find that as you sever the roots of the plants you are moving, you are severing the roots of the plants you are trying to save as well. Then there is the uneasy moment when you suspect that the major taproot you just cut was, in fact, your telephone cable. There will be the inevitable stamping on branches or wounding of other plants with the swing of your shovel. The weather, the time of year, the kind of plant and how long it has been growing in one place will all make a great deal more difference to your success than the perfection of the technique employed. Just keep in mind that if you leave all the plants crowded together, none of them will ever look good, and some will probably die. The bottom line is that either you move it or you lose it. You are not risking much more than a few hours of your time and an aching back, unless you really do cut off your telephone.

I do attempt to practice what I preach, however reluctantly. In our small herb garden are clustered many of our earliest shrub plantings, and they offer perfect illustrations of youthful horticultural folly. The *Euonymus alatus* proved not to be "Compacta" and even with ruthless pruning is taller than I am and several times as wide. There was a globe arborvitae, numerous low juniper species, a slow-growing weeping crab apple, two *Juniperus chinensis* "Pyramidalis"—in short, the typical garden-center selection for unwary beginners, all jammed into a space the size of a living room. One by one the smaller bushes were sent to farther corners of the landscape, with, I must say, a remarkable rate of success. But the upright junipers remained, more and more massive each year, dominating the space with their dense columnar forms and their astonishingly prickly surfaces, a bush to avoid brushing at any cost. One was tight up against the enclosing wall and safely out of the way, but the other seemed to be smack in the middle of several paths and every view. After roughly eighteen years with us it was well over ten feet tall and more than a yard wide: we decided late one Saturday afternoon that it had to go. Did I follow all my careful instructions? Well, the roots had snaked under a stone retaining wall and mingled with those of a more desirable juniper, so many of them were lopped off. Because of the tree's massive size, it was not at all clear that we were going to be able to move it, even if we took it bare root, which turned out to be the case. Once the tree was down (and that part alone took several hours), we found that two of us could move it no more than a few inches. I finally ended up pulling it out of the garden with a car; it took a four-wheel-drive truck to drag it uphill to its new and final resting place, where a few neighbors helped to get it upright in a hole. All this effort may seem absurd; we could have cut the tree down, we could have left it alone, we could have been more prepared for the project. All that is true. But it is also true that the change is infinitely for the better. The herb garden has new vistas, new light, a wonderful openness. The poor juniper is an absolute knockout in its new, uncrowded location. It will probably be a year before we know if it will survive, but at least for now it is a change for the better all around. If we had waited to do it right we probably never would have been crazy enough to do it at all.

Instant-gratification overplanting is only one reason you may have to move plants. Sometimes you simply have the wrong plant in the wrong place. We have all laughed at the Blue Spruce Syndrome. Fifty years ago many homeowners were enchanted by bright blue baby spruces and planted them in front of their houses, only to find, decades later, that they had trees fifty to eighty feet tall consuming their front lawns. But our amusement has not kept us from making similar mistakes. These days, Canadian hemlocks are frequently used in the same way, tucked in next to foundations or beside doorways, in spite of the fact that this is a magnificent—and fast-growing

—forest tree that will reach one hundred feet. It is likely that by the time you realize your mistake, the tree will be far too large for you to move by yourself, but it can still be moved with proper equipment by landscape professionals. One garden designer I spoke with routinely moves trees thirty to fifty feet tall. There will be considerable expense and trouble involved, but you still have a good chance of success, and even failure is better than giving up use of your front door.

When deciding to move a major tree, for whatever reason, consider its rate of growth and value as a specimen. For instance, there is almost no reason to move a willow tree, since they are so inexpensive to propagate and quick-growing that it is better to start over with a young tree and plant it where you want it. Pines, spruce, and fir, on the other hand, are painfully slow for the first ten years, then take off quickly, so if you have husky young conifers inconveniently placed, it is worthwhile to try to move them now. (Sad to say, American hemlocks are now afflicted by an insect pest that can cause death in several years, something to consider before moving or planting one.) One factor determining a plant's survival after moving is how long it has been growing in a place before you dig it up. A specimen planted five or even ten years ago has a much greater chance than a tree or shrub that has spent a generation in one place. You are well-advised to move your own mistakes, but you may have to face cutting down those of gardeners who came before you.

You may be startled when you first try to maneuver the root balls you have made. A bush that barely reaches your knee feels like it is made of lead when you try to lift it; you can't believe it is not still rooted to the ground. Strong and preferably young assistance is a great aid, but even teenage weight lifters are not going to get far with more than the smallest trees. Your best friend in this situation may be a local backhoe operator. He need not be a landscape specialist—the process may be cheaper if he isn't, and for much of your basic lifting and moving, horticultural expertise is not essential. If you accomplish the careful tasks of digging and wrapping, a backhoe can dig new holes and move and place a specimen in surprisingly short time. It is wonderful to see how deft these machines can be—you may be inspired by them to take on major earth-moving projects—but their use applies to large properties rather than to crowded lots, where a big machine could barely turn around.

What about some of those big old shrubs that have been there forever and make the front of your house look like Sleeping Beauty's castle? You may want to keep some of them as sentimental favorites, but you would like to get them back to a reasonable size and shape. A good number of these old-fashioned favorites can be treated with surprising severity and still survive. Old lilacs, forsythia, mock orange, honeysuckle, bridal wreath, and many other specimens can be cut back to the ground and recover. This is a terrifying prospect for some gardeners: if you want to hedge your bets, or your hedges, cut out the largest, tallest trunks within the mass, then cut back the rest by one third or one half. When you see how quickly the shrub recovers, go at it again next year. You can get rid of an old shrub and keep it too: if you want to preserve a special deep color of lilac or a particularly fragrant mock orange, dig out and replant a few of the numerous suckers growing around the roots. This will produce a shrub of manageable size in a few years in a part of the garden where you can use it.

Propagation skills can be a big help when you get down to those difficult decisions about what has to move. If you can reproduce some of your choice, slow-growing favorites, it makes it less terrifying to move the original plant. I recently spoke with a landscape designer who had planted, in his own garden, a rare form of hemlock too close to a magnolia. The magnolia now has a trunk four inches in diameter and is over ten feet tall; the hemlock, if lost, will be irreplaceable. A perfect illustration of a tough decision, and it can happen to even experienced plantsmen. He has taken cuttings of the hemlock and has a few small plants coming along, so he is now prepared to take the risk for the good of both the hemlock and the magnolia and his garden overall. You may not have had much interest in propagation in your first years of gardening, but you will discover more and more what an important tool it can be. If you feel that you are hopeless at it, you might be able to get some help from a local nursery.

Available: Free Kittens and Azaleas

YOU WILL NOTICE quickly that moving plants out of their original location is only one part of the operation. Now what do you do with them? This may be the chance you need to develop other parts of your property. You might want to replace an unsightly fence with a hedge or screen of plants. Large, tough trees and shrubs can be used as windbreaks to shelter exposed areas where less hardy plants can then be grown. Think of them as colonizers, going into the outback of your yard and trying to make it livable. Rhododendrons and their shade-loving relatives can be used as underplantings beneath tall deciduous trees. I find them much more attractive in this kind of natural setting than cowering against a foundation, and you may find, if you live in a harsh climate, that they are easier to grow under these conditions.

If you don't have a place for excess trees and shrubs, or if you are just sick of them, local landscapers may be willing to take or buy them. Community gardens are frequently delighted to obtain well-grown specimens at no cost. Garden clubs, botanical gardens, and other horticultural organizations often hold plant sales to raise money and are eager for donations—

they might even come and dig out what they want. You may be amused to find that the plants you have come to loathe—those with the most lurid blooms, the most bizarre foliage—are the ones in demand.

There are, unfortunately, always going to be some trees and shrubs that must be sacrificed. It may be difficult, at first, to achieve the necessary ruthlessness, just as it is hard to throw out all those *Scientific American*s. But it is exhilarating to get control over a landscape that may have been sliding toward chaos and exciting to see a garden that was slumped in midlife torpor take off in a new, more energetic direction.

Too Many

IT IS NOT always our miscalculations that result in plant overload. Nature can be generous, sometimes to a fault. The problem with trees and shrubs after a decade is their size—at least they are usually conservative about increasing their number. This is not always the case among the herbaceous plants. Remember those early days when you carefully set out three of each perennial in the border? How did those three suddenly become fifty? How overjoyed you were when a neighbor offered you the iris she was inexplicably discarding. Now that you have a truckload of rhizomes yourself, you know why she was even happier to give than you were to receive. You were once so grateful for those pretty weeds that popped up and gave some body to your new plantings: buttercups, Queen Anne's lace, musk mallow. Today some of your double-dug borders are indistinguishable from the side of the road. Did you ever think there could be such a thing as too many flowers? As one of my gardening neighbors said with a sigh, "I never thought I'd see the day when I would pull out a daisy."

But pull we must—the reasons why are blooming all around us. We may have plenty of flowers, but there is a good chance they are not the ones we want. Golden glow and black-eyed Susans seemed charming the first few seasons, with their energetic burst of gold, but now that golden glow occupies all but a few inches of what you once thought of as a mixed border, you are ready to shriek at the sight of yellow. That lovely little blue bellflower that you rescued from the roadside is in fact *Campanula rapunculoides,* which by now has carpeted hundreds of yards of your land. Once it proliferates, nothing but the most powerful weed killer will get it out.

It is easy to underestimate the fecundity of plants until you have been gardening for several years. If you started out with tender annuals like marigolds or petunias, you have no idea how big a herbaceous plant can get in one season, or how wildly it can reproduce. Maybe you are the kind of careful gardener who quickly clips off the seed heads as soon as the flowers have faded, and you have at least some of the problem under control. But many of us, especially in the first few years, *want* more plants and sprinkle seed over any bare patch in the landscape. There are those tricky-to-transplant annuals and biennials you hope to encourage to reseed, like poppies. I remember shaking out the fat gray pods of *Papaver somniferum* and ending up with a garden that looked like the opium fields of Afghanistan. Even if you managed to keep seeding under control, some species have another dodge and produce underground runners to send plants to distant corners of your beds. "Runners" are aptly named—*Oenothera fruticosa,* the golden sundrop, comes streaking through the garden like an Olympic half miler.

It is rather a delicious problem, having too many flowers. But if all this bloom doesn't result in the garden you want, you need to start sorting it out. You now have several times the amount of plant material you had when you started, even allowing for the plants you have lost. You will have even more when you get around to dividing some of the massive perennials that undoubtedly need it. So why is it that somehow more is amounting to less?

There are some plants we enjoy so much that we are almost happy to have them take over the garden. It is fine to have great numbers of a few flowers, but you may need to reorganize them to make the most of their impact. Rather than having them underfoot in every part of the yard, use them in a great sweep in just one place. If a plant is in front of us everywhere we turn, we stop seeing it, no matter how great its beauty. But a mass of it in one place really turns it into a star. You may once have enjoyed the carefree movement of plants across your garden, but now you might prefer to give the impression that someone is actually directing traffic. One way to do this is to declare areas off limits to certain plants. In my garden, the perennial yellow foxglove, *Digitalis grandiflora,* has great success; it would take over most of the county if I let it. This is a lovely plant, with a long period of bloom in cool areas and a soft, warm color that combines well with a virtually unlimited number of other plants. It grows in sun or shade, dry or damp, self-sows eagerly, and is an excellent cut flower. Sounds like the perfect plant, right? That's why I ended up with several thousand of them. It got to the point where all you saw for a few weeks in June and July was yellow foxgloves. I have never really gotten fed up with them, as I have with some plants, but I finally decided to restrict their range. They can romp through the lower, rocky areas of the garden, but I keep them out of the perennial beds where I want a greater variety of plants to be noticed.

Many big, aggressive spreaders are best isolated in one part of the garden. There is a moment in spring when we would be delighted to have the huge oriental poppies everywhere we look, and that seems to be the poppy's secret agenda. The brilliant orange blossoms make a spectacular show, but it is a brief one, and it is better to have them settled where they can be ignored once they are finished. At the other end of the season, the tall New England asters are superb en masse in autumn, and are best kept to themselves so they don't wipe out less aggressive growers early in the season.

No matter how entrancing a flower is, it shouldn't appear to be all we can grow. Use your dominant perennials to characterize just one part of the garden, as you would use one color or pattern of wallpaper for just one room in the house. Sure, your day lilies will grow practically anywhere, and you can scatter them among the shrubs or dot them around the border, but think how striking they might be in a space of their own—a space where you can focus on one kind of plant and see the enormous variety possible within the limits of one species. The tall bearded iris are sensational used in great numbers all together, rather than mixed here and there with other perennials. When you started out, you probably didn't have enough of any one plant to think of turning a whole bed over to it, and you probably didn't know which perennials would do well in your garden. Now you know, and you probably have an oversupply of at least a few species that can step out of the ensemble and do a solo turn. The contrast between mixed beds and mono-plantings can bring welcome variety to the perennial garden.

Back to Nature

REDISTRIBUTION OF OUR flowers is important, but it doesn't solve the problem of too many plants. It is clear that there are still lots of things we should get rid of. Let's start with those lovely weeds that so obligingly showed up in our beds. They may have been useful in the days when you could still see the dirt between the plants, but now that space is at a premium they must go back to the roadside from whence they came. Getting out the obvious weeds is hard enough—how can we bear to dispose of some of the really nice plants that have grown a little too well? Before we start hauling them off to the compost heap, why don't we see if there are other ways we can use them in the garden. You may have all the perennial beds you can handle right now, so let's consider some low-intensity alternatives to the border.

You probably read about naturalizing when you first started out. You may even have tried it, probably with daffodils. The definition of the term may have been a bit vague, as were instructions about how to do it—some catalogs urge us to throw bulbs across the lawn like a game of boccie. There is no hard and fast definition, but naturalizing generally means using plants outside beds and borders in an informal way, a way that we secretly hope will require no work. This should not be confused with native plant gardening, because many of the plants we may use are not natives. We are not attempting to re-create a natural environment or habitat; we are trying to find plants that will suit themselves to the habitat we've got. We know that we have some flowers that do well, almost too well, in our gardens. Let's explore the limits of their tolerance. Naturalizing is actually just a euphemism for "no more cushy life in the border."

I'm sure you know by now how well daffodils do in almost any situation; there are a lot of other bulbs that will be just as successful outside a bed. Snowdrops, crocus, scilla, and *Fritillaria meleagris* are ideal in any area where the grass can be left long until the leaves dry. Ipheion spreads starry constellations across the lawn and is hardier than most gardeners think. *Endymion hispanicus* runs rampant in shady places. *Allium aflatuense,* only slightly less spectacular than *Allium giganteum* and much easier to grow, will thrive in light shade among shrubs or under small trees. Colchicum will provide bursts of springlike, crocuslike blossoms in fall and continue until a hard freeze. All of these are desirable plants for any garden, and none of them needs to be taking up precious bed space.

It is possible that you tried and failed at naturalized planting early in your gardening life, especially if you were misled by visions of yourself broadcasting seeds like a figure in an Impressionist painting. If you were simply flinging seeds into random corners of your yard, it's no wonder you met with little success. You didn't know then which plants would grow aggressively in your climate and situation. You may even have been unaware of what your climate was. You may not have understood what situations lend themselves to informal planting. But now you are much more prepared to make naturalizing work. You probably have your property more under control than you did in the early days. You know which plants have the urge to dominate the landscape and, better still, you have enough plants with which to experiment.

You are sending your plants out to fend for themselves, and they will have a much greater chance of success if you prepare the ground first. Clear away weeds and grass, remove large rocks, and turn the surface of the soil. Naturalizing often works best in lightly shaded areas where grass cannot compete and the number of weeds is limited. Consider the "between" parts of your property: where the lawn meets the trees; where the grass expires before it gets to the garage. If you are setting out perennials, leave them in larger clumps than you would if you divided them to go back in a border. When trying to establish biennials, such as foxgloves, hesperis, or matricaria, move both first- and second-year plants. Encourage self-sowing by allowing seed heads to mature, then scatter seeds in the area. A mulch will give the naturalized emigrants a head start on other weeds, but leave open soil in some patches where seeds can germinate.

Identify parts of your yard that might suit different kinds of plants. A soggy spot where the mower always bogs down might be used by big clumps of Siberian iris or *Iris pseudacorus*. That place under the apple tree where the grass struggles could be perfect for a variety of primroses. One friend disposed of excess dianthus and thyme by scattering them along a gravel road bank in front of the house, where in spite of winter plowing and the dust of traffic they make a show for the neighborhood every June. It is hard to be very specific about which plants respond best to naturalizing, because a plant that is a weed in one region can be a prima donna in another. Even from one garden to the next it is rash to generalize—I cherish my purple echinacea, which has barely spread in ten years, while ten miles away it fills a roadside meadow. You know what are weeds for you—see if you can find creative ways to use them in your landscape.

Naturalizing allows us to enjoy the luxuriance of too many plants without being overwhelmed by them. It also gives us the opportunity to bring flowers to more distant parts of our landscape. The intense demands of border plantings require that they be near the house, under our watchful eyes, within reach of hose and spray gun and deer protection. Naturalizing creates more distant vistas and fosters the impression of the bounty of nature spilling out in all directions.

Even very successful naturalizing will work for only some of your extra plants—you will still eventually end up with too much. You may have luck passing off some of your excess to gardeners just starting out—I smile as I drive down the road to town and see my yellow foxgloves thriving in four or five yards. And the same outlets I suggested for your woody plants might also welcome perennials—community gardens, plant sales, garden centers. Some of the native plant societies have a laudable program that helps out overstocked gardeners and shares the results with those less fortunate. Society members divide and replant desirable perennials for those too overwhelmed or too timid to do it themselves. One manageable segment remains with the owner; one chunk is divided among those doing the work; and one division is used for propagation of plant-sale material to benefit the society. A surprising number of backyard gardeners have started out selling off their excess plants and found themselves in the nursery business. The rest of us must try to cultivate some ruthlessness along with our hardy species, because as long as we are gardening, plants will become bigger, and some will become more plentiful. Some must necessarily enrich only the compost heap, and even there they resist our control—the mound of rotting vegetation may eventually be graced by orange poppies and a foxglove or two.

....

Once we start moving, shifting, and discarding, we may feel a whole new excitement about our gardens. We have plants to spare, so we can feel free to indulge in more daring possibilities, to go beyond the safe and familiar forms we followed when we started out. We can be rash and foolish and devil-may-care because we will no longer feel that the entire garden is at stake if some plants don't make it. In general, we tend to think of youth as the time for rashness, but the youthful gardener is rash only in ignorance—for the most part, young gardeners are far more conservative than those of us who have been at it a decade or more. The mature gardener, backed by a hefty bankroll of plants he would be only too happy to get rid of, can be a real high roller. This new spirit of recklessness will expand not only the geography of the garden as we reach out for new worlds to conquer, but also, less tangibly, its tone. In the second decade, gardening becomes an adventure.

3

Too Little

. . . .

Although THE MIDLIFE garden is burdened by an excess of some things, it can also be characterized by too little of others. We may have noticed the same pattern in the rest of our lives: more around the middle, but a decided thinning on top; more domestic tranquility, but the absence of romantic adventure; more friends, but little chance to see them. In the garden we may be overwhelmed by plants, but discover that they are not the plants we want nor even the plants we planted. Where are the snows of yesteryear, and the numerous shrubs that seem to have vanished beneath them? Why is it that every spring seems to start with a harvest of labels that no longer belong to the living? I will save until later a discussion of what might have been, those "sins of omission," as we said in my Catholic childhood, that might contribute to unnecessary gaps in the garden. But let's start, painfully, with those we have loved and lost, with some of our more tangible disasters.

In gardening, as in life, we all have different notions of what constitutes a mistake. We discussed some typical beginner's mistakes in the last chapter: overplanting, the right plant in the wrong place and vice versa, variations on too much and too many. But these are sins on the side of generosity, mistakes we can be proud of, in a way, because they develop from our success in making things grow. How much more difficult it is to face the opposite. There is no getting around it: a dead plant is a mistake.

Sometimes, of course, we barely notice that a plant is gone. It may just be a herbaceous plant that never came back after the winter or one that dwindled slowly over several seasons until it reached the point of invisibility. Eventually we may come upon the label and recall that, in fact, there did used to be something else growing here.

Shrubs and trees don't go quite so gently into that good night. They can leave a gaunt skeleton that never leafed out, or, after leafing out, a gaunt skeleton hung with limp red or yellow then finally dry leaves. Evergreens can turn a dramatic red brown—I have been complimented on an unusual foliage specimen that was, in truth, a quite ordinary plant made special by its death throes.

It may be hard to face a mistake that is as emphatic as a dead plant. When you come to think of it, death is a topic avoided in most gardening books, or addressed with the kind of euphemisms employed by funeral parlors. But plants don't pass away; if they did, we wouldn't have to dig them up to get rid of them. So while we are digging, we may try to learn something from the plants we have sacrificed to our ignorance.

Plant Postmortems

WHEN WE STARTED out, most of us knew nothing about plants and how to grow them. We bought sick plants. We picked good plants and planted them badly. We planted good plants and they grew and then succumbed to a pest or disease we knew nothing about. We planted good plants that were wrong for our climate or wrong for the particular situation in which we planted them. Many of those mistakes were unavoidable at the time, but are avoidable now if we learned from our fatalities. Our youthful failures may be long gone, but I bet most of us can remember quite a lot about how things went wrong, even if we couldn't figure out why. Doing a plant postmortem on a specimen that died years ago is like trying to reconstruct a crime without a corpse, but we don't have to convince a jury—we just want to convince ourselves that we can do better next time. Of course, we probably have more recent disasters around to examine, too, since one of the facts of gardening life is that no matter how much we learn, we continue to kill plants.

A plant postmortem is a snap for readers of detective fiction—they know all the right questions to ask. Did the plant die immediately after planting? Were there obvious signs of assault, and to what part of the body? Did the end come quickly, or only after a slow decline? What suspects had both motive and opportunity? Slowly we can assemble a case, and even if we end up accusing only ourselves, at least we can try to understand what happened.

Did the plant die immediately after planting, in spite of adequate watering? If so, the fault probably lies with the plant and the people who sold it. This was a much more common situation when trees and shrubs were balled and burlapped. Plants could be dug up with hardly any root, have soil shoved in around the trunk, and be tied up in a sack for the unsuspecting. One advantage to container planting is that the plants usually have been living in their containers for quite a while. They have developed a complete root system within the pot, which suffers less shock than those of plants newly lifted from the ground. (Of course some so-called container plants are just dug and shoved into plastic pots with some dirt and can suffer the same damage as badly handled balled-and-burlapped material.) The only ways to avoid initial disaster are to look carefully at the root ball or container of a plant before buying it and to deal only with reputable nurseries. Even then, there will be unexpected failures from undetermined causes that are collected under the term "planting shock." For example, a plant that became badly dehydrated at some point before it was sold might show signs of that damage only after you buy it. Any plant that dies soon after planting should be replaced without argument by the seller. You may have made any number of mistakes when planting new material—the hole may be inadequate, the soil may be terrible, drainage may be nonexistent, there may be too much sun or too much shade. All these factors will take their toll eventually, but usually not right away. Watering, however, is crucial in the first weeks and months after planting—you may now realize why most of your successes lie within reach of the hose, and many of your failures lie beyond it.

If the plant did well the first season, made new growth, seemed settled before winter, and was dead the following spring, the chief suspect will be climate. First eliminate the possibility of assault—examine the trunk and branches for signs of girdling by mice, rabbits, or deer. If the top of the shrub or small tree appears suddenly to have received a neo-Nazi haircut, deer have probably been at work, especially in winter and early spring. I won't go into detail about conducting war with the creatures around us— after five or ten years of battle, you are sure to have developed your own techniques. Although we all lose valuable material in those first years of assessing the enemy, we should not be deterred by these setbacks from trying the same plants again once we have assembled our defenses: plastic

trunk guards, burlap wrapping, chicken wire, bird netting, rifles, large dogs, sixteen-foot-high electric fences. We may feel at times as if we are trying to garden in a war zone, but we can prevent a great deal of injury when we learn to recognize the assailants and figure out what works against them.

Visible winter injury looks different from animal attack: the bark splits up and down vertically rather than in a ring around the stem. That kind of injury isn't always fatal and it doesn't always occur in winter damage. Sometimes there are no signs other than the obvious deadness of the plant. You might belatedly check the estimated hardiness of the plant in *Hortus* or a similar reference source. If the plant's zone number exceeds yours by more than one (you are Zone 5, the *Sequoia sempervirens* was Zone 8), lack of hardiness is a prime possibility. It is not the only one, and it is not a final verdict, but in our early gardening days, the most common mistake we all make is to plant something too tender for our climate.

Sometimes a plant appears to have survived the winter, starts to leaf out, may even bloom or try to, then collapses. This is often another manifestation of cold injury. Sometimes when root or stem tissue is damaged the plant has enough stored food to make a start in spring, but is unable either to manufacture more or to move nourishment through the stem. Some plants can take the cold but are hurt beyond recovery by frost heaving that occurs once the ground starts to warm up. This kind of damage can be fought with better drainage and heavy mulching.

Even though inadequate watering is the most frequent cause of plant death soon after planting, too much water is another leading cause of fatalities, particularly during the first few seasons. Some plants need more water than others, but very few shrubs or trees are happy with persistently damp soil at their roots. We are all instructed to check the drainage of a hole before we plant anything in it, but there are dry springs as well as wet ones, and a location that appeared well drained in a dry season may turn out to be boggy in later years. Winter drainage may vary dramatically from summer drainage, and excess water freezing and thawing can cause injury in a variety of ways. Drainage, unlike climate, is something we can change, and a species that failed once from this cause might be grown successfully somewhere else on the property.

Other problems show up more slowly. Even a serious incompatibility between your soil and the preferences of your plants—you planted blueberries on a limestone escarpment—will not cause the victim to keel over at once. Rather, there will be a general slow yellowing followed by leaf drop. The bush may even try to produce a new set of leaves and struggle into another season before the problem is fatal. Less dramatic soil insufficiencies will appear even more slowly, often typified by no more than a steady decline. Lack of fertility can be noticed in many of those plants often described as "heavy feeders": roses may grow energetically the first year, languidly the next, then settle into a sulky, semicomatose state. All these deficiencies can be corrected, some more easily than others, as we will learn later.

The plants we kill are not only the plants we planted. It is hard not to feel guilty when some previously long-lived specimens begin a rapid decline the moment you come into their lives. Sometimes magnificent trees that have survived the depression and two world wars come to grief the moment we start paying the mortgage. One of the most frequent causes for this kind of disaster is our urge to upgrade the property: improving driveways or paths, creating patios, making terraces where once there were slopes and vice versa, installing a swimming pool. Any of these so-called improvements can bring about dramatic and frequently fatal changes in drainage patterns. Perhaps the construction seemed safely distant from your plantings, but any change at the soil surface can either direct excess water to areas that were previously well drained, or keep water from flowing out of these areas. Many mature trees cannot tolerate changes of this kind. Trees are not hasty creatures, and especially in our early gardening days, we may not notice they have taken a turn for the worse until conditions are irreversible. Make extensive drainage studies before any construction project gets underway, and consider seriously whether a new patio or path is worth the price of a sugar maple that was young in the days of George Washington.

Ever-Multiplying Suspects

MANY INSECT OR disease problems won't be evident for the first two or three or more years. One reason for this is that insects and the damage they cause are cyclical. New gardeners are often smug when reading about pests and diseases because such problems haven't occurred in their gardens—yet. A new garden can bring plants into an area for the first time, and insect populations take a while to discover this opportunity. Just give them a few seasons to catch on. Insects are often very specific about their hosts—until you grew columbine, you probably never saw a leaf miner, and even within the genus, some species have them, some don't. Probably the leaf miners weren't too bad for the first few years, then suddenly you hit a peak in their cycle when weather and population density and predator cycles all combine, and some of your favorite aquilegia are gone forever.

Fungus problems can develop the same way. Who knows anything about mildew or botrytis in those early innocent days? And they may take several years to become a cause for alarm. But then, after feeling you were the world expert in delphiniums, you look around and see nothing but twisted, blackened stems. One damp summer and suddenly your phlox look as if they're covered with snow.

Some insect and fungus problems are superficial nuisances; some may eventually prove fatal. Some are the former in one climate and the latter in another—you won't know until you have experienced a few fatalities. These assaults can be depressing in the short run. When new gardeners start to experience such failures, their natural response is to turn to the vast arsenal of insecticides and fungicides available in any garden center. These quick fixes are effective against a specific problem for a limited period of time. But the question is: Do you want your garden to depend on weekly applications of poison? The answer really depends on how you see your garden. Do you think that a garden is made only to yield a product, like vegetables or roses? If so, you may find that deadly sprays and powders are an important part of your regimen. But a garden that is a landscape, a place of beauty, and a part of our lives does not have such a specific goal, and the process of creation and constant re-creation does not depend on just one plant or on a single effect. There may be a few special plants you will do anything to grow—fine, as long as there are not too many of them. But for every plant that has an incurable problem, there are five that could replace it. You should feel that the botanical universe offers far more possibilities than you will ever have the room to pursue. The bugs have just given you the excuse to give up on some losers and move on to something more exciting.

In fairness to the insects, you should notice that they seldom completely wipe out their hosts, even in bad years. They may make their victim look awful, they may keep it from blooming for a season, and they may make you wish the plant had died, but they don't usually kill it outright. (Insects or fungus diseases can weaken the plant so that it succumbs to other causes, of course, which makes your postmortem even more of a challenge.) But if you can control yourself through a bad season and keep from tearing out your hair and your plants, you may find that several years go by before you have such a bad season again. This is the tolerant long view that develops after a decade of struggle, especially if you have a great variety of plants and a certain amount of inertia. There will always be a few specimens having a bad year, and enough other glories so that you will hardly notice.

It is not always easy to determine whether an insect, a fungus, or a bacterial or viral infection carried off your plant, which is one reason attempts at treatment may have been haphazard and ineffective. Benomyl is not going to stop caterpillars, Sevin is useless for mildew, and a surprising number of gardeners, not all of them beginners, seem to think that one or the other is a cure-all for anything. Bacteria and viruses are hard to diagnose, in many cases, and even harder to cure. Some result in a quick death, some gradually debilitate the plant over a number of years. There are disease problems specific to one genus and specific to one locale. Diagnostic challenges bolster the argument for having samples of your sick plant analyzed by your local agricultural extension agent, who ought to be familiar with the problems found in your area. You may not want to follow the prescription the agent has to offer if it includes a battery of noxious sprays, but at least you can find out whether you have a problem you can live with, or if you should give up and cut the patient down. Because bacteria and viruses are so difficult to treat, much of modern horticultural science has been devoted to finding species or cultivars that are resistant to the most common plagues, and it is worthwhile seeking these out. If you do have specimens that have succumbed to a wilt or a blight or a rot, as these plagues are variously titled, cut down and burn all remnants and don't immediately replace these specimens with the same or a closely related species.

Not Long for This World

THERE ARE SOME trees and shrubs that are simply shortlived. This is a shocking discovery for many of us who think of thousand-year-old oaks and bristlecone pines and imagine that a tree lasts forever. Under ideal circumstances trees can last a long time, but we forget that many of the plants around us have, according to nature, no business growing here. If we yank a rose species out of western China or a pine out of the Himalayas, we should expect that if it will grow at all, it may not grow the way it did in its original situation. Lombardy poplars are a good example of a classic beginner's mistake. Throughout France this tree lines avenues with pillars of green and gold. Its exclamation-point shape is irresistible as an accent, and its rapid rate of growth recommends it to many neophytes who want a big tree quickly. But no matter how well they perform in Europe, in America these trees are destined for an early grave, and if you have shaped your landscape with them, you had better begin planning for replacements. You may get one that will live for twenty years—ten to fifteen is more usual. In America this tree is attacked by diseases it doesn't experience in Europe, and after looking great for ten years and miserable for five, it will probably snap off in a storm. It is a valuable tree for an instant effect, but you should know what to expect.

In many areas birches suffer similar decline, although over a longer period. The white-bark American species are beautiful northern trees. They will grow well south of their natural range, but in warmer climates they are afflicted with a legion of insect pests. They seldom die immediately, but they can look awful in a bad year and they don't live nearly as long as they do in their own habitat. So birches are a bad bet as a framework or important focal point of a garden. I have seen the flowering almond make big old bushes in many parts of the country, but in my garden it lives about ten years. After six or seven years it starts to develop the black-knot fungus that is a scourge of prunus in the region. It is such a pretty species and blooms at such a valuable time that I am resigned to replacing it as soon as it starts to head downhill. I do the same with the sour cherry trees, which suffer from the same problem. In all these cases, and many that you will discover in your own roster, fungi or diseases or a combination of both result in a shortened life for certain desirable specimens. They may have a long and happy life someplace on the globe, but cannot be thought of as long-term residents in all gardens. This is no reason not to use them and enjoy them for a while, but we must try to arrange things so that they leave no awkward scars.

Herbaceous plants may be even less reliable in terms of longevity and life cycles. In my brash early years in horticulture, I was astonished to find that many practicing gardeners apparently don't know an annual from a perennial. Of course, the more I've learned about habits of growth, the more complex they appear. Oh, for those early days of clarity when I could believe wholeheartedly that all plants lived for one year, two years, or forever. As you get to know more plants, you find that so many of them resist these simple descriptions that now, when someone confidently describes a plant as an annual, I am inclined to inquire cynically, "Where? And for whom?"

Climate and culture both have enormous impact on habits of growth. A species in its natural location may be primarily annual or perennial, although even in the wild plants don't keep perfect cycles. Move a plant to a different climate and it will often adjust to its new location by changing its habit of growth. A longer or shorter season, the presence or absence of a dormant period, more sunshine or less, longer or shorter days—all these factors can influence when or how a species will bloom and how long it will live.

Besides the changes a plant might make to adjust to life in a new locale, there are numerous changes a gardener might make to get a specimen to bloom at a desired time or to grow in a place it might not otherwise survive. Read an English seed catalog if you want to experience some of the variations to be made on the annual-biennial-perennial theme: "A half-hardy biennial best grown as a hardy annual if started early." "A short-lived perennial grown as a hardy biennial." "A slow-blooming annual usually treated as a half-hardy biennial." The permutations are endless and hilarious, but they are the well-intentioned quibbles that result from centuries of gardening experience and they reflect the diversity, or perversity, of the botanical universe. They also reflect the great flexibility of the English climate. A great many of those so-called biennials are not going to make it through an American winter. Some laid-back annuals might get around to blooming in California, but cannot be coerced into a ninety-day growing season, no matter how early you start the seeds.

I seem to digress from our theme of garden fatalities, but these various habits of growth may actually explain some of our early failures in the border. Even when they are called perennials, some plants just don't live very long. A plant that is long-lived in cooler climates—the hybrid delphinium is a frustrating example—may act more like a biennial in the South or California. There are short-season biennials that turn into annuals in warmer climates. Some species, like lupines, are notoriously short-lived in soil they don't find to their liking. Some monocarpic species, those that die after flowering, may appear perennial over the several years it takes them to reach blooming size, but then they infuriate us by dying as soon as they set seed. We can manipulate these factors to a certain extent once we understand them, and occasionally succeed where we failed in our early days. But it is even more important to realize how variable the factors are. We are not the first to find a hole where *Aster frikartii* bloomed so brilliantly last season. We will not be the last to mourn the departure of fleeting fritillarias or quixotic campanulas. A plant does not have to be permanent to earn a place in the garden; in fact, many of our best-loved specimens are the most ephemeral. Knowing that some choice species are not long for this world gives them the piquancy of tubercular heroines of the nineteenth century and can spare us some unnecessary guilt.

The Shades of Day Are Falling Fast

SUCCESSFUL TREE PLANTING can, after a decade, demonstrate clearly how we can achieve simultaneously too much and too little. Of course we are thrilled as our previously arid and overheated landscape gradually matures into a series of green and leafy glades. Not so thrilling is the gradual loss of the sun-loving flowers and shrubs that once made up our plantings. The progress toward darkness is often so slow that we hardly notice it, but other inhabitants of the landscape are more acute. As the shadows lengthen, stems become longer, leaves turn a paler shade of green, flowers become smaller, then sporadic, and finally absent. We may be gaining a forest but we are losing a garden.

Much of the United States is natural woodland and many properties are well—often too well—shaded. Gardeners in these areas learn to live with shade from the outset and enjoy it by employing the many shade-loving plants that are native to our woodlands. But the gardener who starts with full sun often doesn't give shade a thought. Given the wealth of plants that need lots of light, he plants trees, shrubs, and flowers here, there, and everywhere. The fleeting shadows cast by saplings amount to nothing in those early days, so most trees are surrounded by bulbs or perennials. Little by little the trees grow and spread, until those early pale penumbras are dark wells of welcome shade, and the once-bright borders are lanky ranks of anemic and attenuated starvelings.

Few conditions seem easier to analyze than the difference between light and dark, but it may take a surprisingly long time to realize what is causing your problem; the change in light is subtle and occurs over a long period, and it has many manifestations. We may think that lack of fertility is the culprit and it is, indirectly, since the plants may not have enough sunlight to manufacture the nourishment they need. But extra feeding will not help the long-term problem, and it may simply feed the tree or shrub that is casting the shadow. Watering patterns may have to change. Even though the soil is not exposed to direct sunlight, less rainfall can penetrate the umbrella of the tree overhead, and the ever-stronger tree roots will be competing for water as well as for food.

As with so many of our crises at this stage of our gardens, recognizing the problem is the first big step. Then you can begin to figure out which trees will permit companion planting, and which are complete black holes. The diaphanous light under a locust, for example, is sufficient for a wide selection of plants; late-leafing fruit trees can accommodate a rich assortment of early bulbs; heavy-headed shade trees like maples and large evergreens eventually eliminate light like a blackout curtain. Slowly but surely the plants will sort themselves, but you may want to avoid further fatalities and rescue some favorites to move to sunnier locations. If you want to maintain plantings under some trees, you will have to change their character completely to adjust to your new woodland situation. Congratulate yourself on your happy trees, and move those miserable flowers to brighter and greener pastures.

The Day of the Living Dead

However sad it is when something dies, it can be even sadder when something doesn't. At least death is final—you can dig up the corpse and plant something else. But how much more wretched are those plants that clearly don't want to live, but don't want to die. These are plants that barely start to leaf out by July, are actually brave enough to make new growth by Labor Day, then turn black at the first touch of frost. These are plants that after two years of feeble growth suddenly produce a suspiciously vigorous set of shoots that have leaves, flowers, or fruits utterly unlike what you originally planted. And how about those shrubs that spray out scrawny arms four or five feet high but only bloom at the bottom three inches? Or those plants that retreat rather than advance in size?

For a few years you may admire the will to live that keeps a plant growing when it is clearly miserable. Perhaps you even congratulate yourself on your superior cultivation that makes it persist against all odds. These plants are like the enormous tortoises in zoos—they aren't really living; they are just taking an extraordinarily long time to die.

After killing off a number of plants inadvertently, it may be hard to face horticultural euthanasia. It is easy to stall: maybe this year will be milder; maybe it needs more time to settle in (perhaps ten more years?). But the misfortune of these mistakes goes beyond a small blot on your landscape. These sad relics are the lessons you are refusing to learn. By keeping them around, you are insisting that you are right: that you don't really live in Zone 4; that your soil *is* acid enough for blueberries; that roses don't need full sun; that taxodiums shouldn't mind a dry spell or two. It is true that some plants are hardier as they get older, and if you get them through the first crucial years you may have success. But after four or five years you have to make an assessment of your selections and stop nursing along specimens that long for *requiescat in pace*. You will be amazed what a lift it will give your whole garden to be rid of these ghosts.

What about the case of the mysterious new growth that appeared from the roots of a shrub you thought had died? Many plants of dubious hardiness are grafted onto a rootstock that will survive greater cold. Very often, when the grafted plant dies, the rootstock sprouts and grows. The rootstock may produce a healthy and hardy plant, but it won't be the plant you wanted, nor the plant you paid for. It will very likely have fruit or flowers inferior to your original choice. If you have space to spare, you may decide to keep it; but if you need to be selective, these plants are often not worth growing. Also keep in mind that a rootstock may produce suckers even when the grafted top is still alive. Since the rootstock is often more vigorous than the graft, the suckers can overwhelm the top. Keep an eye out for changes in foliage, bark, or flowers, especially if they are produced on long, straight, fast-growing branches from the base. These should be cut off as close as possible to the ground or the trunk.

Where Have All the Flowers Gone?

SOMETIMES IT IS not just a single tree or shrub that vanishes, but a whole area of your garden. Where, for instance, have all the wildflowers gone? Not the wildflowers that were here when you moved in, but those brilliant tapestry-like meadows you once sowed in generous handfuls across the landscape. The Meadow-in-a-Can and its early competitors were a marketing triumph, but for many they were a gardening disaster. Even those lucky enough to have success the first year were seldom still pleased after the second, and after three or four years all that was left of the idea was a patch of invasive grasses and a few oenothera. The myth in a can was that you could sprinkle seeds like fairy dust pretty much anywhere and great patches of wildflowers would spring up in your wake. Most experienced gardeners could only gape in disbelief at this idea, which is why the seed mixtures were originally sold through nongardening gift catalogs. The horticulturally innocent were entranced by the idea and made it one of the record-breaking seed items of all time.

If planted with some degree of care—e.g., good soil preparation, watering, and weeding—the Meadow-in-a-Can could produce a pretty splash of color. But it was hardly care free, and it was hardly a meadow. For one thing, the so-called wildflowers were wild only in the sense that all flowers were wild once. They consisted mostly of European annual poppies and bachelor's buttons, perhaps with annual flax, foxgloves, and oenothera thrown in. On an open patch of ground with no competition, these flowers would succeed for a season; if you kept the weeds down, you might even get a second year. But these species simply can't compete with native grasses and forbs, and if you spend enough time struggling against the inevitable, you might as well be working on a flower bed in the garden, where these plants belong. In spite of all the negative aspects of the myth in a can, it did, in a somewhat roundabout way, do a great deal for gardening. It was a low-anxiety way to interest nongardeners in flowers in the landscape. People who panic at the idea of working out a whole border could be comfortable with the notion of a wild mix of color and shapes that seemed to happen more or less by chance. And it got people interested in the idea of wildflowers, if not, initially, in wildflowers themselves. After the disappointment of the disappearing meadow, some converts to horticulture wanted to find out what flowers would actually make a meadow work.

Our wildflower landscape has become so saturated with aliens that it is hard to be a purist, especially if you just want something that is lovely to look at and easy to manage. Oxeye daisy, musk mallow, crown vetch, Queen Anne's lace, red clover—pretty though these species are, they are not native Americans. They will, however, contribute to a meadow that will be some-what more enduring than the original Meadow-in-a-Can. If, after your disappointment with that fiasco, you still want to reconstruct the missing meadow, study the fields and roadsides around you. Do some research to discover the native field flowers in your region. Look to see what your local highways can teach you—many highway departments have made an effort in recent years to establish wildflowers on roadsides and median strips. In your garden you may have a number of plants that are too successful for the border and would be better reintroduced to the wild: rudbeckia and ratibida, the brown- and black-eyed Susans in all their variety; echinacea;

solidago, all those glorious goldenrods; coreopsis, gaillardia, verbascums, and oenotheras, the vibrant orange milkweed, species lupines, and varieties of penstemon. You will have a much greater chance of success if you start with plants rather than seeds. Not a lot of soil preparation is necessary, but sod layers must be broken up and preferably removed. You will want grasses in your meadow, but not the kind you have in your lawn. Bunch grasses like *Andropogon virginicus, A. scoparius (Schizachyrium scoparium), Panicum virgatum,* or *Sorghastrum nutans* are lovely and less likely to force out the forbs. If you want to add more interesting regional specialties, there are now far superior seed mixtures available that consist only of natives. You can recapture that lost meadow, if not the carefree innocence with which you first sowed it. And if it isn't exactly care free, it can still be a beautiful way to use flowers.

Even a meadow of native wildflowers and grasses cannot be considered a permanent part of the landscape in most parts of North America. Except in the prairie regions of Middle America, an open field of herbaceous plants is merely a stage through which the landscape passes on its way to climax vegetation, which is usually some form of forest. You may think that you will have more than enough time to enjoy your meadow while waiting for hardwoods to displace it, but in fact the character of your field will change rapidly if you don't intervene. Smaller woody plants move in almost at once: fast-growing brambles, shrubs, small trees. In three to five years, what was once a meadow can become a sea of scrub. If you want to keep your meadow, you should be prepared to fight for it. Yearly mowing or overburning will give your wildflowers the edge they need.

....

This catalog of catastrophe may not have accounted for all your early disasters, but perhaps it has offered insight and consolation for a few of them. It would be even more consoling if I could say the worst is over, but that is not true. In the early days we mostly killed easy plants, plants we had every right to expect to grow. We can go back and grow them again—this time, perhaps, with success. But now most of us want to go beyond the plants that everyone can grow. We begin to long for plants we have never seen, plants with no common name, plants that have never ventured into our climate. Some of these experiments may broaden our horticultural horizons, but they may also expand our R.I.P. list. Death is a forceful teacher of the limits of our own knowledge and it has shaped our gardens as we have learned from it. As we garden more, we discover that death has lost some of its terror, at least as it pertains to plants. We no longer feel the paralyzing remorse that once marked the discovery of every corpse, that made us swear we would never lift another shovelful of dirt. We know that there are plants we have no right to expect to grow, but at times we cheat the odds, or the climate, or conventional wisdom, and succeed. In those moments we feel like the heroes in fairy tales who gamble with death and win. We can flirt with disaster; we can sport with mortality. We may lose interest in plants with too tenacious a hold on life and court instead the young Werthers of the seed lists—*Eritrichium nanum, Androsace helvetica, Campanula arvatica*—plants so bent on their own destruction that even having a good-size corpse is a badge of distinction. Death may eventually have the last word, but until then we may learn to live with it.

4

Sins of Omission

....

There IS A terrible moment in the Christian liturgy when we ask forgiveness "for what we have done, and what we have failed to do." How awful to be held responsible not just for doing the wrong thing, but for not doing something we might never have thought to do. This can easily become part of our self-assessment during a midlife crisis, as we speculate about the jobs we might have taken, the men or women we should have encouraged, the children we didn't have. Some of these options are closed to us now, and many are better left unexplored. There are paths not taken in our gardens, too, but some of the possibilities we overlooked the first time around could enrich our landscape now and are certainly less likely to get us into trouble than speculating about what it would be like to be a firefighter in Alaska or wondering whatever happened to that cute guy who used to save you a seat on the school bus.

Our gaps in the garden can extend both through space and through time. The spatial gaps are easy to find once we start looking. There are the obvious holes where something died and you have finally brought yourself to remove the body. But there are more subtle spaces that may not have existed when you first started to plant. Small trees have become taller trees, with inviting opportunities for planting underneath. If you have succeeded in clearing out some of your excess shrubs, you could carpet the open areas between what is left with bulbs and ground covers. When we start to plant a garden, so much of our material is little and close to the ground it never occurs to us that someday we could encourage a whole layer of bloom where once there was only mulch. Underplanting is a neglected possibility for many gardens, particularly small ones that can't expand horizontally. Think of all those underutilized square yards beneath the rosebushes, for example. You could enjoy months of early bulbs followed by blue waves of forget-me-nots, which are then replaced by fragrant mats of annual alyssum, carrying on until the last rose of summer—quite a change from the present pile of wood chips.

In some cases, we may have planted ground covers that have roughly as much interest as the mulch they replace. In terrible soil and no sunlight, we may have to be satisfied with lamiastrum or English ivy, but with even a little more to work with, we could be growing primroses instead of pachysandra.

Underplanting expands the range of the garden without expanding its size. It gives us a chance to look through one plant to another, to play with size and scale on the vertical as well as the horizontal plane, to use colors not just by parading one next to another in a border, but by building up the delicate layered washes of an aquarelle. Underplanting gives a role to likable plants not important enough to hold center stage, like polemonium, epimedium, or *Symphytum grandiflorum,* which in spite of the Latin is not grand at all. It can camouflage personality disorders in lily of the valley or early anemones, whose leaves go to pieces after flowering. Best of all, it gives depth and subtlety to even mundane areas of the yard and leads us to believe that every corner contains a possibility, every overhanging branch conceals some wonder.

When you are tired of looking down and under, consider overplanting. There are vines that could grow up and over the trees and shrubs you already have. There are areas of vertical opportunity you might have overlooked. Not just obvious arbors but the walls of sheds or garage, even the house, could be gaily decked with climbers. You might be wise to keep stranglers like wisteria away from your more delicate architectural features, although for sheer luxuriance of bloom and extravagance of perfume it is hard to beat that anaconda of the plant world. Climbing roses are irresistible in warmer climes, especially the early profusion (and lack of thorns) of *Rosa banksia.* Those of us in the north will have to be content with the hundred or so varieties of clematis that flower between April and October. These can twine around trees or trail down banks, cling to conifers and shower dowdy shrubs with flowers the size of water lilies. Just this one genus can add a layer of bloom to almost any garden. One of the beauties of overplanting with vines is that it can unite the vertical with the horizontal by carrying the movement of flowers up out of a bed into the trees. Vines give a rich sweep to even immature plantings and soften the harsh edges of new construction with lush curves.

There are sure to be gaps of this kind over and under almost any garden, opportunities you have not yet explored for expanding both the range of possible plant material and the places in which it is used. Consider the thrill of trillium clustered under dogwood, the astonishment occasioned by *Arisaema sikokianum* around the enkianthus. Underplanting and overplanting, in different ways, develop modes of planting we may have been unaware of when we started out, back in those days when we thought that a perennial's place was in the border.

Replanting the Calendar

LET'S GO ON to more subtle lapses. It is not hard to have a pretty garden from May to July (April to June in warmer zones). After a few years you could lose half the flowers that bloom in June and no one, including you, would even notice. In fact, you probably *have* lost half the flowers that bloomed in June and didn't notice. But what about the other months of the year? Some of us are so concerned with filling minute blanks in the border that we don't notice that the biggest blank extends from October until March. Of course, readers from Florida and California are exempt from this accusation, since it is almost impossible to maintain legal residence in those states if you don't have something blooming year-round. But the rest of us need to work a little harder to fill up the calendar.

One encouraging part of planting for those so-called dead months is that it takes very little to create a sensation when you have limited expectations. This is best illustrated by the impact of the snowdrop. The snowdrop is not what you might think of as a sensational plant. It is short and white, and it faces down so that its lovely interior markings and poignant fragrance are lost on those unwilling to lie on the damp, cold ground. This would never be a hit in June. In February, however, it is a sight to make the heart leap, a thrill that makes a sortie into the desolate yard worthwhile. It is unlikely that you are not growing snowdrops, but are you giving them the attention they deserve? Surely there are places in light shade where they might be planted in hundreds. You could try some of the different species and their many varieties, including a double that might make you believe double flowers can be beautiful. Snowdrops bloom for a long time, so they are well worth the effort, and if they are the only show to open the year they might as well be a good one. They are not flowers of which one tires.

In spite of boasting the name of Christmas rose, *Helleborus niger* blooms nowhere near December except in the warm states. In my northern garden it is useless, because it doesn't unfold its demure, ground-hugging blossoms until May when it is outshone by almost everything. *Helleborus orientalis,* more realistically styled the Lenten rose, is a much more valuable landscape plant, with striking foliage, easy care, enormous tolerance for shade, and flowers that look great for two months. This sounds too good to be true, but more and more garden designers are discovering that it is, which has given the understated hellebore considerable vogue. Although the flowers are not flashy, they are fascinating—speckled and spotted, in deep rose or icy white with greenish tints. What appear to be petals are bracts and never

actually wither; they just turn more and more green and eventually disappear as the seeds are produced. They will bloom in January or February in many parts of the U.S. (in March in harsher zones), and they survive late frosts and unexpected snow. Even if they didn't bloom so early they would still be valuable as an underplanting, carpeting areas beneath trees and large shrubs. They take care of two sins of omission at once.

The snowdrop and the hellebore are examples of plants that are useful because they fill a specific gap. They have little competition during their hour of glory, so their somewhat subtle charms attract our full attention. Anything that ventures aboveground in early spring is worth a try: tiny, brilliant species crocus, which are weeks ahead of their overblown hybrid relatives; resilient early *Iris reticulata* or *Iris histrioides* and their variants, so delicate in appearance and so tough in the face of frost and snow. Have you overlooked eranthis, which look like short, fat buttercups with ruffs around their throats? Consider cyclamen for very late fall or early winter bloom, depending on climate and species. Eranthis and cyclamen are both excellent tucked in under shrubs, or carpeting areas in light shade; the cyclamen are

as desirable for their foliage as for their early bloom. Although most of us grow tulips, many seem unaware of the fascinating species, some of which bloom almost as early as crocus and in a rainbow of colors: *Tulipa turkestanica, T. humilis, T. biflora, T. pulchella,* and *T. sylvestris*—these are just the beginning. There are many species from exotic locales, and great care should be taken to determine that the ones you buy are not harvested in the wild. More than enough are offered by reputable growers, so you can enjoy these little tulips without subsidizing the destruction of natural populations.

In among those early tulips and the first narcissus it is a treat to find clumps of pulsatilla preparing to bloom: the unopened blossoms look like down-covered baby birds huddled in a nest. Slowly the stems stretch and the petals unfold to reveal deep purple surrounding a medallion of gold. This easy, hardy perennial should be as common as the daffodils it accompanies, but it is still an underrated plant. And once you have your fill of the many shades of purple pasqueflowers, go on to discover the red, white, and glowing yellow. *Pulsatilla vulgaris* is the most available and comes in many color forms: *P. halleri, P. vernalis, P. patens* are a few of the many species to pursue. Fluffy seed heads succeed the flowers and last for months.

The above suggestions may not be new to you, but you should consider whether you are making the most of your earliest blooms. Like snowdrops, all these little bulbs and perennials should be used extravagantly so that they show up in the bare, early spring landscape. None of them requires choice bed space, so they are not usurping the place of later, important perennials. Many of these early apparitions are considered, for better or for worse, as rock garden plants. For worse, because some gardeners believe that rock garden plants are weird or difficult or otherwise off limits. This absurd idea has kept many from enjoying all the easy species that could add weeks of bloom to their gardens. None of the species mentioned above needs any special coddling. Of course, if you do become interested in the more abstruse pleasures a rock garden has to offer, you could look forward to golden mats of draba, silver masses of saxifrages, and the soft, spiderweb spread of androsaces, to name only a few.

Not all our early delights are close to the ground, and not all are for the eyes only. The spring-flowering witch hazels are graceful shrubs or small trees, with gold or bronze blossoms and delicious fragrance in the early months of the year. The native *Hamamelis virginiana* is less showy, but equally fragrant and hardier; it brings its unexpected fruity odor to the air in late fall. Chimonanthus is not showy, but its pervasive perfume in January is a powerful argument for growing it if you are in Zone 6 or south. *Lonicera fragrantissima* is as fragrant as its name implies and will grow as far north as New York City, where it blooms in March. It is much more valuable in warmer areas like Washington, D.C., where it scents the streets in January and where its semi-evergreen foliage doesn't look so dog-eared in winter.

We all sigh longingly over the "winter garden" chapters in English garden books, or accounts from our own writers in the South or on the West Coast. There is no point in yearning for that kind of plenitude in most of the U.S. through the winter months. But once we have made a garden and long to be out in it during every season, it is gratifying to have a few items of interest to get us through the shortest days. We read a great deal about "seasonal interest" when we first start to garden, but it doesn't mean much until the landscape starts to fill out. "Seasonal interest" is a vague, catch-all phrase, in any case. It usually means whatever we start to notice when nothing is in bloom. One of the solaces of maturity is that we notice more of the details around us; we see nuances we might have overlooked in the haste of youth. More practically speaking, many subtleties, like bark color and twig shape, don't really show up on a sapling three feet tall. After ten years there simply is more to notice about our plants, even in the off-season.

Most of us first plant *Euonymus alatus* for its startling foliage, which certainly enlivens a few weeks of autumn. But as the plant grows, we may come to love its winged twigs in winter—first hung with astonishing fruit, then bare or outlined in ice crystals. The whole show of red leaves and brilliant berries goes on for at least two months; you have hardly tired of the twig effects when you notice the new pale green leaves appearing. Altogether, it is a plant of abundant seasonal interest.

Ilex verticillata is rather the opposite, a plant that is completely nondescript until the moment when you need it most—in dark November when there is nothing to look forward to except Christmas. Suddenly, like a Christmas ornament in the wild, we see the vibrant red berries along the black twigs of a shrub that has become a showstopper overnight. The fact that it is extremely hardy and thrives in swampy soil are further incentives. And out there in the swamp with the winterberries, you might plant the red-twig dogwood. Or one of the red-twig dogwoods—confusingly, there are two species, one American, *Cornus sericea,* one Siberian, *Cornus alba,* and many cultivars of each, including ones with yellow twigs and several with variegated leaves. These accommodating shrubs have in the last decade become darlings of the landscape trade for exactly the reason I mention them here—they fill a gap. After Christmas we badly want to see something other than bare branches. It may be months before the first flowers, especially in the north, so if we have to look at bare branches they might as well be red. The twigs of this dogwood are always some shade of crimson, however muted, but at a mere hint of longer days, the branches flush with tints of Chinese lacquer. There are hybrids that are redder than red, almost too shocking when we see them in a nursery, but in January, against frozen ground and frigid sky, we are only too glad to be shocked.

Evergreens are the examples always given to illustrate seasonal interest. In a young garden they might not offer much proof to support the claim. In my yard, to avoid winter deer damage the first few years, the choice dwarf conifers were so heavily swathed in burlap and chicken wire they looked more like works by Cristo than living plants. And there is only so much interest to be found in even a rare chamaecyparis if it is the size of a soccer ball. There are those who argue that evergreens don't get more interesting in winter, they just benefit from the fact that everything else gets more boring. But some of your conifers may make a real show in winter by now. You might notice, among their more subtle delights, the opalescent shades of the junipers, the thick clusters of cones at the tops of even small white spruces, the sparkles of resin dotting the bristlecone pine. My favorite conifer for seasonal interest is not evergreen; every season the larches are dramatically different. In summer they are clothed in soft yellow-green needles; in fall they turn a stunning gold weeks after the other deciduous trees; in winter their bare, chestnut-colored branches are arching, knotted sprays of miniature cones, irresistible for Christmas decorating; in spring the new needles burst in whorls from the twigs, recalling countless Japanese paintings. Now that is seasonal interest.

Another aspect of seasonal change in the landscape is to be found not in the details but in the visual masses, the volumes we have arranged around us. Areas dominated by deciduous trees or shrubs become light-filled and transparent, taking on a completely different character from that which they display in warmer months. Evergreen parts of the yard become much more forceful. This shift of emphasis is a subtle but fascinating part of the winter landscape and one we can reinforce by building up the size and variety of evergreen plantings.

Timing Is All

A RICHER, MORE interesting landscape does not necessarily mean more plants or great numbers of plants. It means finding the right plant for the right moment. You have lived for years now in your garden. You have begun to feel the rhythms of your landscape, its ups and downs; every garden has them, just as nature does, and sometimes it only takes one plant to create excitement and pleasure at an unexpected moment.

One way to supply interest is to shift the spotlight from one plant form to another. The usual pattern of bloom proceeds in spring from early bulbs to flowering trees and shrubs, to later bulbs, then later shrubs and perennials and biennials. You probably don't need any more trees that flower at the same time as the crab apples, but a large tree that blooms in June, such as the catalpa, can be a pleasant surprise. This was a popular tree from the thirties to the fifties, then dropped from nurseries, probably because it is somewhat messy. It has large flowers, large leaves, and wonderful long hanging beans, all of which fall and annoy the fastidious. (Local children will try to smoke the beans, which are somewhat less harmful than most of what they could be trying to smoke.) Its annoying features give the catalpa that old seasonal interest, and the great mounds of flowers late in June make a spectacular show.

Another June-blooming tree is not so spectacular, but it is one of the best hardy shade trees. The European linden, *Tilia cordata,* lines avenues in many of the world's great cities and is extolled in countless lieder. The first time it blooms, you will understand why, as its heavy, seductive odor blankets the summer landscape. In New York City, the tough olfactory competition notwithstanding, the perfume flows out of the parks and spreads like honey for blocks. The bees banquet for weeks on this tree, and elderly European ladies gather the flowers for an insipid medicinal tea. Considering that the little-leaf linden has one of the most perfect rounded crowns of any shade tree, it is mysterious that American nurserymen prefer to sell cultivars like Greenspire, which are more vertical and not so nice. The linden flowers as late as July in the northern parts of the U.S.

You may think it impossible to have overlooked any gaps big enough to be filled by a large shade tree, and if you have a very small yard or a tree-filled landscape, that might be true. But many of us would like to find room, because we are becoming more interested in trees as we grow older. This seems ironic, as if the young and stalwart have the monopoly on large plants simply because they are somewhat more able to move them around and because they might live to see them in maturity. In fact, the stages of gardening interest often start with vegetables for young, often very young gardeners—those endless numbers of preschoolers who have sprouted radishes and lettuce, started potatoes in jars of water, watched lacy leaves shoot from the tops of carrots. Annuals are usually the next area of interest, followed by perennials and shrubs, and ending, in middle age or later, with a fascination with enormous and often slow-growing trees, many of which are available only from seed. This is not necessarily sensible. It would be much more reasonable to establish the outline of our garden first with woody plants, which would be maturing while we filled in the details. But true passion, for plants or anything else, is seldom sensible. A love of trees implies both patience and an appreciation of the joys of delayed gratification, neither of which are attributes of either young lovers or young gardeners. As a result, many of us find ourselves late in life in pursuit of esoteric forms of aesculus or the tempting cultivars of sorbus, confident that somehow we will find a place for them, once we get them to germinate.

After this digression into the Several Ages of Gardening, let's return to our quest for seasonal surprises. Most shrubs flower in spring and early summer, so the long strings of pink or white flowers on the clethra, the sweet pepper bush, would grab our attention in August even if they didn't possess their intoxicating, narcissuslike scent. It is easy to grow tired of our gardens by August, and the sudden infusion of freshness from this leggy native of the Northeast is most welcome. Rose of Sharon is an old-fashioned favorite that makes the most of its somewhat dowdy charms by displaying them in September.

By September or October our attention has begun to shift back to trees as we look forward to the fall foliage show. At this point we can hardly remember what our early crocus looked like, so colchicum and autumn crocus seem almost surreal as they pop up in the autumn landscape. Colchicums produce sturdy, straplike leaves early in the season, but these wither and disappear and by October we have usually forgotten we ever planted these unusual bulbs. Carpeting lightly shaded grassy places, they create a dramatic effect as the orange and red leaves from overhead drift down around their amethyst cups.

Arum italicum won't stop traffic like colchicum, but it is another gap-filler that works on two levels: its striking, marbled leaves unfurl in October and remain striking through the winter; it can be used under dormant shrubs that will look like nothing for those months. It is a detail plant, a treat for those who like to hunt for treasures, something to make us wonder what other little-known delights of the green world we might have overlooked.

You might be forgiven for overlooking the ghost bramble, *Rubus lasiostylus var. hubeiensis,* since this spectral Chinese native is a recent introduction from the Sino-American Botanical Expedition in 1980. If you are looking for something out of the ordinary to light up the dark winter days, the six- to eight-foot-tall canes make a startling, spiny, bright silver accent in the silent landscape. Many of the lovely rubus species are only fantasies for those who garden north of Zone 6, but this one has been thriving at the Arnold Arboretum in Massachusetts, so it is well worth a try.

These are all random examples of plants that fill the gaps, that work against the familiar patterns of our expectation. It is difficult to make too many specific recommendations, since we each have different rhythms in our gardens. What is a gap for some is already overcrowded for others. Timing is crucial: you might search out a certain tree said to bloom in July only to find that in your climate it flowers in early June with everything else. Visit friends, relatives, and total strangers in your area to see what they have blooming when. Local display gardens and arboretums are helpful in leading us to that one plant that could make a difference.

I may be overcautious about making assumptions about other people's gaps because my own garden has had some major lapses I have only recently begun to fill. After the first spring rush of bulbs and rock-garden specialties, I found that in early May, although I had many plants in flower, I needed something to provide impact. I had lots of blue and pink and purple, crowds of camassia and drifts of fragrant hesperis, but I needed something with a strong, defined shape and a bright color, something to give a focus to the garden at that time. The answer was so obvious I am almost ashamed to reveal it. I needed red tulips. Tall red tulips. For years I had been telling people not to plant tulips—they get eaten by everything, and they don't come back reliably, and they are probably one of the most banal and overused plants in North America. But once it was clear what was needed, I resigned myself to planting tulips and protecting them every year, and from there it was only a short step to loving tulips, banal though they may be. I have forsaken all the pretty decorator shades and now seek out only the most ferocious, tulips with names like Easter Fire, Red Shine, and King's Blood.

Just as I have become resigned to the extra effort of tulips, we all might find that we have to work a bit harder to ensure the presence of a few special plants. When we first read about biennials, many of us decide that they are just too much trouble. Why give time and space to a plant that does nothing for one year, then blooms and dies the next? The answer can be found in the majestic beauty of foxgloves, in the sturdy, velvet mounds of sweet william, in the furious orange colors and beguiling scent of erysimums, the hardy wallflowers. Each of these has a character that is distinct and irreplaceable. To them I would add two oddball biennial favorites of my own. *Oenothera hookeri,* a western native that appears modest when it begins to bloom (on July first in my garden for the last eight years), can reach over three feet in height and width by the time it is cut down by heavy freezing.

Every night just before dusk it unfolds large fragrant pale-yellow flowers so quickly you can see them open. Another yellow stunner for midsummer is *Verbascum* "Silver Spire." This is a hybrid form of the common mullein, but instead of a single column of flowers it produces a many-branched, five-foot-tall candelabra from a substantial rosette of silver, felty leaves. Both these biennials are drought-resistant and self-sowing and provide unforgettable moments at a time when both garden and gardener feel a bit dull.

Great Expectations

IT IS EASY to carry on with lists and accounts of our individual triumphs, but these shouldn't be taken as overall recommendations. Rather, they should urge us to go through our gardens, looking for soft spots, seeking those moments when we feel no urge to go out of the house, those weeks when we feel we might as well go away. These are the gaps to work on, the ones no one might notice except ourselves. No garden is ever fully realized in the mind of the creator, but a richer, fuller landscape is one that makes us feel that we can hardly bear to leave for even two days—not because the lawn needs to be watered, but because we are afraid we will miss something.

Anticipation is such a powerful sensation that it is surprising it is not written about more often. How much of our enjoyment of an event lies in its expectation rather than in its actual occurrence? How much of the excitement of youth develops from the anticipation of the adventures to come, all the sensations to be experienced? How much of the depression of middle age develops from the sense that there isn't much to look forward to? It is anticipation that makes our response to spring so strong: although the garden will be more beautiful as we move into summer, it will never have as much promise as it does in the early weeks when all our hopes are still intact and all the inevitable disappointments have not yet taken their toll.

We all want something to look forward to, and this is the purpose of paying attention to "sequence of bloom," although it is seldom explained that way. We have all come across this phrase, with its detailed calendar of floral events designed to ensure maximum flowering in our gardens at all times. (I even have an old book entitled *Sequence of Bloom in America*.)

Although it is often supposed that the ideal of a garden is to have flowers in bloom all the time, what we really want much more is to know that flowers will be coming into bloom all the time, which is quite a different thing. The Victorian carpet beds, and much of public gardening around the world, consist of masses of annuals set out, in bloom, early in the season, which will then remain in full bloom until frost. That gives you a garden full of flowers, but it does not give you anything to look forward to. The garden in September is only a slightly taller version of the garden in June, which is usually why we stop looking at it around the Fourth of July. In such a garden there is no reason to go rushing out after a few days away to see what has happened in our absence. There is no anticipation; nothing is going to happen except that at some point it will all be over.

Having a lot of flowers in bloom is not enough. It is thrilling for the first few years when we are uncertain that anything will grow. (In fact, I still retain my awe and gratitude for the way things grow.) But now we want new plants coming into flower for the first time; we want to see changes in the landscape from week to week; we want to think there are still pleasures awaiting us even as we approach the end of the season. We don't need quantity to satisfy this craving—after the riches of the early season, we can be satisfied by just a few beauties. We don't even need flowers, specifically. We may hardly have noticed the blooms of false Solomon's seal, *Smilacina racemosa,* but it is a thrill to discover the beautiful opalescent berry clusters that slowly turn red through the fall. *Actaea pachypoda,* the white baneberry, also has a quiet flowering at a time when it is easily overlooked, so the bizarre "doll's eyes" berries are all the more startling when we find them in September.

Anticipation is the reason to have some annuals starting late so that we don't grow tired of them, the reason to have some summer bulbs, like acidanthera, that don't begin until August. It is the argument for the late-flowering clematis, trailing through parts of the exhausted landscape so that we can enjoy not only nodding golden bells or snowy banks of stars, but the extravagant seed heads of silver floss that will persist through most of the winter. This is what ought to be meant by seasonal interest: those changes that make each month, each week, in the garden specific, different, unbearable to miss.

All this interest and anticipation does not depend on quantity or even on great variety. Sure, there are times when masses of flowers are a delight, and there are enough accommodating species to make that possible for any garden. But you don't need fifty different kinds of perennials in bloom the first week in June (in addition to the thirty varieties of roses). Replace a third of those June flowers with lilies that will flower in August, with anemones that will bloom in September, with primroses that will open in April. Then you will have something to look forward to.

Southern Comforts

I WRITE, UNAVOIDABLY, with an eye to the northern garden. That is where I live and where I try to garden and where I know the climate best. The rhythm of the southern garden is somewhat different, although the same principles apply: you still want to create anticipation; you still want seasonal interest. But the South has a much longer time frame, so the rate of the transitions takes on a more typical southern languor. It is possible to have a great deal of bloom from January to May, and March and April are times of breathtaking beauty and rich variety. But the summer months can be close to unbearable, and the garden should take account of that. Flowers can be exhausting—not just the effort it takes to produce them, but even the enjoyment of them. There are times when all the color and variety can be like the clangor of loud music when you want silence. A northern gardener, with the rush of a compressed growing season, can hardly understand this until she spends a few weeks in temperatures that seldom drop below eighty-five degrees. Flowers make a great demand on our attention, and it is easy to find them insistent rather than welcome when the weather is hot and heavy.

It is during the dog days that the bones of the garden, the strength of its design and the force of movement through it, are crucial and when they give us the most satisfaction—quite the opposite of how we think of design in the North, which can be all but obscured in summer and is most valuable to us in the nonblooming months. So the southern garden has its pause, its aestivation, in summer. This is when the chief delights derive from masses of foliage, quiet corners, the sound of water, and many places to sit. This is when the gardener should be gathering his strength for fall, which in the South can be a time of glorious richness and extended satisfaction. The North has the drama of spectacular foliage, but we enjoy it with one eye on the calendar as we wait in fear of the first frost. In the South there is leisure to enjoy the subtle beauties of late bulbs, later roses, and chrysanthemums that seem never to die. All too many southern gardens fail to take advantage of this time. Following the northern calendar, they seem to feel that September is the end of the line. Instead, they could be anticipating months of salvias and dahlias, weeks of eupatorium and tricyrtis, the disorienting appearance of the reblooming iris that seems to turn November into May, autumn crocus and cyclamen that will carry them almost into next spring.

....

Maturity, in the garden or out of it, should not bring an end to anticipation. Until you have tried zizia or schizanthus, you can't claim to have seen it all. As long as phyteuma and phuopsis remain in your future, you have plenty to look forward to. We are only beginning to realize all there is to enjoy. We are not even close to the limits of what still waits to be discovered.

5

Refining Design

. . . .

$\mathcal{So}$ FAR WE have limited our discussion to the content of our gardens: what we once had and now don't; what we should have but don't; what we shouldn't have but do. Now we must venture into the subject of form, the ever difficult question of garden design.

Some of us actually worked at designing our gardens, setting them out with grids and slide rules, even if we knew little about design and less about gardens. Some of us called in professionals, turned the whole business over to them, and imagined that we would never have to think about it again. And others were not conscious of design at all but simply began to garden, putting in some shrubs here and there, sticking in a few trees we thought we might like, making a bed for flowers or vegetables when the idea occurred.

It really doesn't matter how your design or lack of it came about. After several years, you may have very different ideas about how to use outdoor space. You can see how your design theories failed to take into account both the vagaries of the plant world and your changing interests in different aspects of that world. Yes, there was a time when you thought roses were a great idea, but here you are with sixty hybrid teas when all you want to grow is hardy cactus. Your first design may not have been strong on problem solving—ten years later you still don't have a place to put the garbage. You understand more about your landscape than you did ten years ago: After years of watching guests cower and umbrellas topple in your windswept seating area, you realize it would be the perfect place to dry the laundry. Even if the garden was designed by a professional, you need not accept as final all the decisions that were made a decade ago. For one thing, plants are not alone in growth and change—the sandbox space could probably be employed more profitably now that your daughter is applying to college. Or you may like the way your garden works overall, but want to clarify lines and strengthen spaces that have become obscured by ten years of growth. You may just be tired of the way the whole layout looks.

Advice on design can seem either disconcertingly abstract or excruciatingly specific, dwelling vaguely on axes and focal points or diagramming in tedious detail the seven ways to park seven cars in your driveway. It is easy to understand why many gardeners are much happier dealing with mildew or soil mix or seed stratification. But even a gardener needs to get in and out of the garden, and family and friends want to stroll and sit and see. Design is a combination of lines and spaces, of movement and rest. We want to create a separate world outdoors, a world shaped by both natural forces and human ideas. Every garden is a different equation between man and nature, between the artificial and the natural. No matter how we balance the equation, we still need design to shape the spaces, and we need design to bring us into the spaces. Assuming that you have figured out how to accommodate the car and where to put the garbage, we will concentrate upon the arrangement of planting areas and the places between them. Redesigning at this stage of our gardening lives may be like rewriting a résumé by selectively ordering decisions and events to create an apparent sense of purpose. We may need to clarify and rearrange the elements we have been living with in a way that makes them appear intentional and coherent.

The Path Not Taken

YOU MAY HAVE a utilitarian view of paths: paths are a way of getting from one place to another; paths are what we make when a bed is too wide to be weeded without stepping in it. You may have the decorative view: paths are ornamental areas of brick or fancy stone; paths demonstrate our skill with edger and lawn mower. Yes, but they are much more. Paths are the means of drawing our design upon the world around us. They are the simplest way to lay claim to the landscape, to shape it, to direct our view of it as well as our motion through it. "Trackless wilderness" refers to the untouched and unexplored, because the track—the path, whether through virgin forest or suburban backyard—is what brings man into the landscape. A path makes everything else possible.

You may not have thought of all this when you started, and even if you did it is possible your paths still have problems. The most obvious is that the paths are too narrow. This is symptomatic of many of our early design mistakes—we are not accustomed to planning in terms of outdoor scale. Even a small outdoor space is much larger than the rooms indoors with which we are familiar, and all paths, gateways, and steps must be larger than their indoor counterparts just to account for this change in scale. Besides that, our pathways must take into account what is growing on either side. A three-foot path that once passed easily through clumps of small shrubs can shrink to the barest deer trail once the bushes are pressing in upon it. Lawns and ground covers encroach, inching over stepping stones until the open space will hardly accommodate the toe of a ballerina. Recently I lost a path completely—an entire stone-paved walk. It was not the only path in the garden, and I continued to go around and about without missing it for some time. This was not one of my earliest efforts, which were always too narrow; this particular path was close to three feet across. But the fierce silver onopordums had set themselves along the edge of it and reached out their spiky arms as they shot up to seven feet, keeping even admiring visitors at a distance. You could still get through if you stayed at strict military attention, but the slightest bend at the waist to pluck out a weed was greeted by a barrage of needles to the rear. Then the annual poppies, which delight in having their roots down among rocks, took off when the traffic declined; the violas and veronicas, only barely under control during the best of times, rose up in multicolored waves until all that was left of my path was a glorious but impossible riot of flowers. A path is not a path, and therefore is not upholding the design of a garden, if it is indistinguishable from a planting.

At least some paths should allow for companionship. Although we seldom go up the stairs or down a corridor two by two in our houses (unless they are very grand), it is one of a garden's chief delights that it can be shared, and shared side by side, if the paths permit. Two people can walk comfortably on a path four and a half feet wide. A standard garden path—one that can accommodate a wheelbarrow—should be at least three feet wide. If the paths are going to be edged with giant thistles or multiflora roses, more space will have to be allowed. A major axis or entrance walk should be over five feet wide. These widths seem absurd when you are first laying out a garden where nothing is growing, but if you have been dodging through your

perennials or sidling sideways among the shrubs, you may be willing to see the wisdom of all that space, even though at this point you may have to start moving plants to achieve it.

Paths should take account of changing weather conditions—are they slippery, unstable, or even underwater after several days of rain? Although your paths do not have to be quite as well drained as your beds, drainage is still something you have to think about. Bad drainage results in puddles in summer, cracking cement and heaving stones in winter. Even a fairly deep gravel walk may need a course of drainage tile under it in low areas. Impermeable surfaces should either have a slight tilt or be raised in the center to shed water down both sides. Keep an eye on the places where the water will go when it drains off—you may simply be moving the puddles off the path and onto the plants, which may not welcome them.

Most of us start out with grass for our paths, since it is cheap and available, and we may feel cautious about committing ourselves to a more indelible garden structure. But there are drawbacks to grass that may be apparent to you now that you know more about your garden and climate. There are large areas of the U.S. where grass can only be grown with regular watering. This is an unnecessary expenditure of time, money, and resources, especially since in many of these areas, grass can look distinctly out of place in the surrounding landscape and would be better replaced with gravel, concrete, or paving. In parts of the country with a suitable grass climate, other problems arise. Any gardener in the Northeast would have been aware of this during one of those summers when it seemed to rain almost every day. The soaked, slippery lawn, although exceedingly picturesque, is profoundly uninviting; I suppose this is why the English have such a reverence for Wellingtons. Another drawback to grass in a climate that can support it is that grass in a green landscape does not provide the visual structure a path can give. One of the beauties of a path is that it directs our eyes—into the garden if we wish, or out beyond it into the larger landscape, or toward some goal not yet visible but desirable because of the inviting path. After directing our eyes and our minds, it directs our movements. Sometimes grass is not emphatic enough to get our attention. If the path moves off from a lawn, we may need something stronger to get us started in the right direction.

It is not necessary that all the path materials throughout a garden be the same. Using only one path surface will give a unity to a garden that might be appealing, but there are good arguments for variety, too. A change in the path can signify different areas of the garden: Gravel might be fine for a shrub walk, but out of place when you enter the woodland garden, where tanbark or wood chips would work better. A mown path seems natural through a meadow, while stone would be the obvious choice in a rock garden. These separate areas may not be large—it may even seem pretentious to call a little shady glade a woodland garden—but having distinctive paths helps to set them apart as discrete planting areas and contributes to the sense of spaciousness and variety within even a small property.

Although we make our gardens mainly for ourselves, we can learn a great deal about the failure of our designs by observing garden visitors. This is particularly useful in seeing where our paths go wrong. We have adjusted our movements through the garden until we hardly notice where we swerve to avoid a limb, where we push past bushes or scramble up rocks where steps used to be. At times my own progress through an area is punctuated by leaps to avoid an unstaked delphinium or hops as I move from rock to rock—tiptoe through the tulips, indeed. I am chagrined when visitors not much further advanced in middle age than myself resist a tour murmuring of knee surgery or the risk of broken hips. Do your guests wander aimlessly from one corner of the yard to another, barely penetrating the planting areas? Do they remain stranded on a rocky ledge and cry for assistance, or scamper across your newly planted lewisias when they have missed a turn? Do you hold your breath and wonder about liability coverage whenever anyone over sixty asks to see the flowers? All these are clues that your paths are not doing their number one job, which is to guide people safely and comfortably through and around the property.

For many people, nongardening people, plants are not enough—they need some more compelling reason to venture into the landscape. A path can provide that reason. Americans in general are not educated garden visitors—they need a garden that shows them how to look. A path can turn an isolated tree into a choice specimen (especially if you put a label on it), clusters of bushes into a shrubbery, that enigmatic English entity. A path changes a forest into a woodland garden with little more effort than simply making it accessible—but not too accessible.

Many gardens develop sporadically around the edges of the house and garage, running along a fence or wall if there is one, with perhaps a flower bed or two erupting from the lawn. Everything is visible and nothing offers an incentive to wander beyond the back step. You know in your mind how it all should fit together and you probably have an established route to favorite plants and recently acquired rarities. But if you do not pull your guests around by the elbow, they will stand on the lawn and "see" the garden with a brief 360-degree glance. A path can draw them into the garden, make them pause for special effects, teach them how to look. You must take the routes that exist in your mind and make them concrete—or stone, or gravel.

No one wants to trot out through the garden and back the same way. (An occasional visiting couch potato might have that inclination, but it is up to you to keep him from giving in to his baser instincts.) Even if you have a strong central axis and a very formal design, it is important to develop alternative routes so that a sense of circulation is established. This can make the most of your planting areas by allowing them to be seen from different directions. The garden of Bunny Williams in Connecticut provides an example of changing points of view expanding the possibilities of a single space. Her perennial garden is a formal rectangle, with big, deep beds at each end and a pool and fountain in the center. The two beds are backed with high treillage, and behind each one is a shady little walk with an urn at the far end. Although the first way you view the beds is from the front, later you might stroll behind and peer out at the brilliant colors and moving water through the cool shadow of the fence. Bunny is a highly accomplished designer and she took an all-too-familiar garden arrangement and made it wonderfully appealing by very simple means.

Avoid the cul-de-sac. We all love the idea of the "secret garden," a small, intimate part of the property with only one barely visible entrance. But most parts of the garden should have at least one way in and another way out, if not more. People are resentful of being lured into a place they can't get out of, which is how they interpret having to return the same way they entered. Perhaps this is a remnant of a primitive instinct to avoid being trapped; whatever the reason, it is noticeable in many visitors. They immediately respond with a defensive attitude: Well, if you're taking me all the way out here, it had better be good. Few garden areas are spectacular enough to overcome that kind of hostile anticipation.

Lucky the gardener whose property provides a strong incentive to move across it, but if you do not have a natural feature that provides a draw, you can always make one. My visitors cannot get to the pond to swim without going through the garden. They cannot get to the barbecue pit or the picnic table without passing the perennials—they may be too hungry to admire them, but at least they have the chance. You can do the same with the swimming pool or tennis court, placing them so that the garden is not some isolated event, but an integrated part of your outdoor life. You may not initially have thought of these areas as connected to your garden, but a convincing path with plantings along it can make it seem as if they were all part of a plan. Another way in which your garden can draw people in is to have it offer an alternative to the terrain immediately around the house. If the house is deeply shaded, let the garden provide a spot of tempting sunlight; a shady woodland is a natural lure away from an overheated patio. Even a small garden needs some kind of lure, be it no more than an arbor or gazebo. A bench, a fountain, a pool, any of these will pull people out of their natural inertia, but it is the path that directs us and leads us on, showing us how to move through the landscape while the garden unfolds its secrets around us.

Questions of Scale

SCALE OR PROPORTION is a kind of Proteus—no sooner do we think we have grasped it than it changes and we have to start grappling all over again. Even Webster becomes uncharacteristically slippery: "Proportion is the relation of one portion to another, or to the whole, or of one thing to another, as respects magnitude, quantity, or degree." Proportion, then, is a relationship, and, as we know, relationships can be satisfying or miserable or anything in between. And, as we also know, relationships change. They are particularly apt to change if some elements of the proportion are growing. Because a garden is made up of growing materials, the spatial relationships we established in our early garden designs have changed considerably over the last five or ten years. Some of our first design decisions were mistakes in scale from the beginning; other errors have developed from our misunderstanding of plants and how they grow.

Scale is what makes your eight-year-old child look enormous next to a four-year-old and, moments later, shrink beside a teenager. If you furnished his room in infancy with tables and chairs appropriate for a creature three feet high, you will one day be startled by the sight of your Brobdingnagian son huddled over a Lilliputian desk. This is exactly what is happening in your garden if you did not understand scale and anticipate growth.

Many early problems with scale arise from our inexperience with the out-of-doors. Most Americans today do not spend much time outside their homes and, when they do, they're usually engaged in some structured activity that keeps them from feeling what it is like to be a human being in the landscape. We spend our daylight hours going from house to car to office to car to house, with perhaps a detour to the supermarket or a Chinese restaurant. We are accustomed to walls and ceilings, to corridors and elevators, to furniture and carpets, and to lighting we can control at any hour of day or night.

Quite a bit of writing about gardens is devoted to the concept of outdoor rooms, to developing metaphors intended to make us see the parallels between indoor and outdoor space. This is reassuring but greatly misleading, because although there are similarities the differences are much more significant, and the greatest difference is scale. We move differently outdoors—our strides are longer, our gestures larger, our voices louder. Distances that would be great indoors are hardly noticed outside. There are no ceilings. We notice immediately what a difference ceiling height makes to our sense of a room, so how do we adjust to rooms whose only ceiling is the sky and whose walls started out at eight feet but now top thirty?

It is helpful to start noticing the differences between indoor and outdoor scale. Look at a building being demolished—how tiny, cramped, and un-livable the spaces appear when they are open, like a dollhouse, to air and sunshine. How flimsy the furniture of a bedroom looks when arrayed on the lawn for a yard sale. And how many of us have made the classic blunder of scale when we cut our own Christmas tree? We attempt to bring an object inside that looks modest, even puny, in the winter landscape. It turns out to be not only larger than any object in our house by a large margin (this is easy to see as the tree effortlessly flattens lamps and end tables), but perhaps even larger than the room where we planned to put it. This is one way to learn about scale in a hurry.

All outdoor spaces must be larger than their equivalents indoors—a space that would be ample for a living room will make only a tiny patio. But besides allowing for the difference in scale when we plan our gardens, we must also allow for the fact that spaces that may have been too small when we made them get even smaller as all the plants around them get bigger. An outdoor room of twenty by thirty feet, surrounded by young shrubs, may be an attractive seating area when you plant it; when those shrubs are six or seven feet high and just as wide, and the seating area has shrunk to a twelve by twenty patch hardly big enough for a chair, you may have to think of other ways to use the space. In some cases, even if the actual dimensions of an area are not diminished, a space will still change in character as the plants within it grow. When I first constructed our herb garden twenty years ago, there was a south-sloping area bordered by low walls that we planted with creeping thyme. Although not large—roughly fifteen by twenty-two feet—it was open and bright and actually seemed to deserve the term "thyme lawn." The dimensions of the lawn have not changed in twenty years, but two knee-high junipers that we planted in it have become bristly columns fifteen feet tall that dominate everything around them. The thyme lawn is still fifteen by twenty-two, but it has lost its identity as a separate space.

Similar transformations may have taken place in many of your early spaces. You may have a number of insignificant planting areas that should be consolidated or eliminated. A small bed of tiny shrubs may not look ridiculous at first, but as the bushes grow and crowd and sprawl, it becomes clear that a larger area is needed. The same thing may have happened to your first perennial beds—you realize belatedly that an area five feet square is barely large enough to accommodate one *Crambe cordifolia,* let alone the sixteen other plants you originally put there. Some of these spaces should be cleared away as you widen paths and strengthen the sense of movement through the garden. In general, your open spaces should become larger as you move away from the house. You may have "borrowed" the scale of the house for a patio or pool deck that adjoined it, but as you move out into the open, human architecture is no longer a point of reference, and the spaces must make sense in the larger landscape.

You may need to reassess the character of some of the areas of your landscape. The size of plants, particularly trees and shrubs, affects our relationship to them and affects how we use them in the garden. This sounds obvious, and it is easy to understand if our garden consists of mature material when we start, but that is seldom the case. Most of us structured our gardens with relatively young plants; small trees and shrubs, when we plant them, seem like decorative objects, rather like furniture in our homes. After ten years these plants have a completely different character, which influences how we move around them, sit around them, and how other objects appear relative to them. A sapling six feet tall looks like a coatrack; it would be absurd to think of sitting under it. But in ten or fifteen years it could be a dominant form in the garden. It will create a specific sense of space that we can use, once we notice the changes that have taken place.

In the early days of my garden we planted a small crab apple, and I immediately made a large flower bed around it. After the first year most of the perennials were taller than the tree; I forgot for several growing seasons that a tree was even there. The lupines were the first to depart, but they are quixotic for many reasons so I paid no heed. A few years later only the stalwart phlox and Siberian iris persisted in the ever increasing shade, along with an improbable delphinium. It shot up in pale blue spires through the branches, even after the tree had achieved the majesty of ten feet and was spreading a cool shadow over a circle ten yards across. At this point the combination of tree and perennials was doing neither any good, since the flowers obscured the shape of the tree and the tree made the flowers look cramped and spindly. It wasn't until I had replaced the tall perennials with ground-hugging, shade-loving primroses that I could see the beautiful, sculptural shape of the tree, which is now the dominant form in that part of the garden.

A great many woody plants go through an awkward stage at this period of their growth. Trees that were pretty little specimens for the first few years may in maturity become lofty and dignified, but there is a decade or so between now and then when the tree is neither big nor small—too big to walk past but too small to walk under. This can be as difficult as living with a teenager. In some cases, as with your teenager, you may have to design around the problem until it reaches the size you can deal with. I have a lovely *Malus* "Red Jade" that wept happily to one side of its path until two years ago. Five years from now, if I am lucky, it will arch up over the path and weep down the other side. But at the moment it is resolutely weeping right down the middle of my axis, and I am weeping in frustration. The path is closed until further notice. Sometimes tactful pruning can get you through a rough patch: this won't work with your teenager since there are laws about such things, but plants are another matter. (That may be why we garden.) You can trim back offending branches until the tree assumes a more mature stance. You can clear out plantings around the tree to give it an impression of greater height—a tree surrounded by faster-growing shrubs will look insignificant for much longer than one given the added dignity of a low ground cover.

This gradual evolution of our garden spaces is one of the beauties of designing with living material, but it is not always easy to predict if we are not familiar with the plants we use. This is one reason why many landscape architects prefer to create a "hardscape" to dictate the major spaces in their design: large areas of paving or deckwork; arbors or pergolas with massive pillars; pool houses and patios. It is easy to envy the walled gardens of Europe; the framework is there, the scale is worked out, the plants within may change, but the design will not. The great gardens of the Italian renaissance were constructed that way—all the important effects were carved in stone, quite literally. Although those gardens do have plants in them, their creators clearly were not taking any chances that the organic parts of the garden were going to get the upper hand. It is helpful to realize that the Villa Lante, for example, was under construction for forty years before it was considered finished. (That's one way to avoid the usual ten-year crisis.)

The combination of our early scale problems and the growth of our plants may have resulted in a garden that seems to have shrunk to half its size. In fact, many gardens at the end of their first decade look as if they should simply be spread out on a lot twice as large as the original. For the gardener with only a quarter acre, this is no solution, so a great deal of digging up and moving out, simplifying and eliminating are the only answers. But many of us did not employ all of our property when we made our gardens, and this may be the time to expand into unexplored territory. When we first start to garden, not all of us are comfortable outdoors. Just as young children or young animals start slowly to explore a new terrain, moving out a few feet and then hastily returning to home, so do we, as adults, move slowly onto new ground. I see this recapitulated whenever we have visitors from the city. Most of them become uneasy if they are more than twenty feet from house or car. They must be coaxed to explore beyond the backyard. Although there is a large pond less than fifty yards from the house, it goes undiscovered unless the timid are led to it.

When we start to garden, most of us follow a similar pattern and concentrate our efforts close to the house. There are practical reasons for this —access to water and tools, greater protection from animals—but I believe that it is the psychological reasons that are most imperative. Many of us simply are not comfortable out in the open by ourselves until we have spent years living in our gardens. After working with a property for ten years, gardeners have a different attitude. Now they are ready to move away from the house and the cramped, too familiar spaces around it.

If you do have room to roam, this is the time to expand. Although you may have a fear of the garden getting too big or out of hand, a cautiously expanded garden can result in less work rather than more. Wider paths of stone or gravel may be a considerable expense to install, but in the long run they will require less care. Larger, simplified areas of grass are often easier to mow than awkward, cut-up patches. Overcrowded shrub beds are no less effort than the same number of shrubs in a space twice the size. You may be spending a lot of time and energy cutting back trees and shrubs that would look better if given a chance to spread to their natural sizes and shapes.

Structures and Structure

THE PROBLEMS OF scale that we had with our paths and spaces could extend to many of our outdoor furnishings. Any kind of structure or furniture must be heavier than indoor counterparts both in appearance and in actual weight; any kind of arbor or pergola must be solid both in its construction and its outline; rockwork must employ large and heavy rocks to be convincing. Not only do outdoor furnishings need to withstand wind and weather, they need to look as if they could withstand it; they require visual force to show up in the open. If they are not overbuilt to outdoor scale, they

will appear as insubstantial as a stage set. Of course, some of these elements may actually be as feeble as they look—how many of us have seen our early arbors wrestled to the ground by the first roses? There are few sights more pathetic than that of a trellis that looks as if it is supported by the plant at its side, instead of the other way around.

Take a hard look at your first walls or rock terraces. Too often they are made of stones that are much too small. Study the walls of your region that have stood for a century—you may ache at the thought of all those rocks, but that is the scale that will not only look right, but will be standing a decade from now.

Constructions like arbors, pergolas, and garden houses, when solidly built and carefully placed, can be invaluable parts of any design, but they do not automatically solve all design problems and they can create a few of their own. Prefabricated models are often tacky in appearance and flimsy in construction. They should not be placed too close to the house, where they always appear a bit nonsensical—why would you venture only ten yards from a big, comfortable house to sit in a little, cramped room? Use these structures as far away as you can to lure people through the garden. It is astonishing the lengths people will go to sit down—make them earn that arbor. All structures should be made in a style that is compatible with the architecture of the house and other outbuildings, or in a style that is characteristic of the region—a rough-hewn Adirondack-style arbor might look peculiar in Charleston, for example.

Even the best-built outdoor architecture needs regular attention. Paint must be kept fresh; boards replaced before the entire arbor starts to sag; posts reset and walls straightened after frost heaving. This is a constant part of a garden's upkeep. A pergola that is drooping and gray contributes only dreariness to a garden; any wobble can ruin the credibility of a wall. Of course a genuine ruin is another story—we want to enjoy the spectacle of its picturesque decay. If you do have such an attraction, perhaps the abandoned foundation of a barn or a springhouse, let your plantings and paths make the most of it. But be very sure it is an architectural fragment worth preserving. We had the remains of a chicken house the size and shape of a good-size motel on our property for many years, ideally situated to be a focal point for the garden. But the only way to bring it into the garden was to bulldoze it and build a lovely small guesthouse in its place. There is nothing the least bit romantic about a ruin of cinder blocks.

Steps and stairways in the garden are as important as design elements as paths and may have suffered from similar design problems. Any change of level in the landscape should be considered a wonderful opportunity for drama, for surprise, for a shift in mood or perspective, or a change in planting style. It is the job of steps to make the most of this opportunity, to emphasize the transition from one part of the garden to another. From a utilitarian viewpoint, steps should be much broader and deeper than those indoors, and they must be solidly built.

It may be that the elements of your design need more emphasis even after you have cleared out the spaces and simplified the lines. Edging can be a useful tool to bring a space into focus. A line of paving in front of perennial beds, a ridge on either side of the paths, brick used to clarify the shape of a lawn or seating area, a forceful series of stones across a gravel court—all of these elements can give strength to a design without necessarily changing its character.

Timidity is the prevailing sin of many early garden designs. You have now lived with your ideas for a decade—if they don't work, change them; if they do work, enhance them. For better or worse, make your statement loud and clear. Give some force to your lines; make your spaces stand out. There is nothing wimpy about nature. If you are tentative in your gestures, they will be lost in the open air. Subtlety is fine for color schemes or plant combinations, but a subtle design is too often no design at all.

Near and Far, Fast and Slow

PLANTINGS AND PATHS combine to influence how we move through and around the garden. Different kinds of plants demand different levels of attention. Shrubbery, even when in full bloom, does not require the same kind of close-up scrutiny as a perennial border. You can move quickly through shrubs or enjoy them at a distance. Paths among shrubs should be broad and comfortable, leaving lots of room for the bushes to reach full size. In any garden, regardless of size, there should be some areas that can be seen and enjoyed at a distance, and others that draw us close. Your plant selection can do much to enhance this sense of near and far. A mixed perennial border seen across a lawn can make the most of such giant flowers as plume poppy, *Crambe cordifolia,* veronicastrum, rheum, the biggest asters, the brightest phlox. This would not be the place for delicate sprays of coralbells or the subtle charms of astrantia. A border of such oversize beauties will be stunning at a distance and draw people to it; it does not have to be seen close up to be appreciated. A rock garden, on the other hand, is seldom at its best seen from afar; at a distance it can look like a jumble of tiny spots. You may have to be close to begin to get interested, and you should move slowly while you are looking. The paths still have to be solid and comfortable and wide enough to prevent stepping on the plants, but they should encourage stopping and peering rather than rapid passage.

You may not have any area of your garden that is as specific as a rock garden, but it is worthwhile noticing what a contrast this type of planting presents to, say, a rose bed. A wide variety of small, unusual plants demands a lot of attention, even from visitors who are not very knowledgeable; it is a "slow" part of the garden and makes the most of a limited space because there is so much detail to discover. A raised bed of small-scale perennials or bulbs makes the best use of flowers that might be lost in a big border. A rose bed, on the other hand, can make a nice splash at a distance. It will make a lovely place to sit, as well, but doesn't lend itself to hands-and-knees examination. These contrasts make the most of your interest in different kinds of plants and make the garden seem rich and varied.

You may have, scattered around your property, many different plants that could benefit from reorganization to emphasize certain characteristics and to set apart the area in which they are planted. For example, you might dedicate one shady spot to authentic woodland plants. You are probably growing a number of plants that could be regarded as shade tolerant, but many of these look as if they are always longing to escape the shadows and get back into the sun where they belong. True woodland species, such as trillium, asarum, jack-in-the-pulpit, cimicifuga, and ferns, to name a few at random, have a visual coherence that is very appealing and that marks off an area as their own. They don't all have to be American natives—there are lovely Asian species that work well here and complement our own. The character of woodland plants will set this area apart from other plantings in the garden.

In this way, unified plant groups can become design elements, shaping and separating parts of the garden as definitively as any architectural elements. I have long thought that this is the appeal of herbs in the garden. Herbs are a fascinating and diverse group of plants, often interesting rather than beautiful. They have, overall, a similarity that sets them apart and they have historic associations that add to their visual coherence. They are plants that invite touching and tasting, pinching and sniffing. The herb garden may be small and limited in scope, it may not have germander edging or santolina parterres, but it exists as a separate entity that is immediately recognizable and adds immeasurably to the richness of the garden.

The Spaces Between

AMERICANS ARE KNOWN worldwide for their inclination to overschedule. "Twenty-one cities in twelve days" was the classic indictment. Now we make conference calls from mobile phones as we speed from one place to another and television shows have four ads every minute. Often our gardens show the same urge toward nonstop stimulation. As we sort out our plant material and rework our design, we should consider the virtues of quiet. Of course we enjoy the thrill of color and masses of bloom; we all still yearn to achieve the ever elusive sequence of bloom. But it can be even more important to have moments and places in the garden where nothing is happening. This can be a clearing in the woods where the path opens out and the light changes—a leafy green passage between two sunny and colorful areas. It could be a spot by a stream with nothing more than a bench and the sound of moving water; the majestic shade of a tree a hundred years older than your house; a corner that the sun warms in winter. If a garden consists only of high points, it will be exhausting both to live in and to visit. For many of us, the garden is an opportunity to depart from our everyday life, yet we often bring to it the same sense of frenzied activity we long to escape.

We can learn a lot about the value of quiet spaces from the great southern gardens of this country. It is true that they reflect a pace of life and an abundance of available manpower that no longer exist, but they also demonstrate an appreciation of the understated pleasures of the outdoors, the satisfactions of sitting in or walking in or simply sharing a green place. It is easy to argue that a grand garden has ample room for such underutilized areas and that in a small property it is necessary to make every inch count. But one way to make every inch count is by providing a contrast to the loud and colorful and demanding parts of the garden, by providing repose in which we can enjoy a more peaceful aspect of the landscape. We need variation in intensity—in our gardens, in our music, in our conversation, in our food. A piece of music that is nothing other than loud can be unbearable; we need not only loud and soft, but sound and silence. Sometimes it is the spaces between the notes that matter most.

6

Border Disputes and Perennial Questions

....

Perennial FLOWERING PLANTS were among the hot and trendy items of the eighties, along with junk bonds. There are, in fact, surprising similarities between junk bonds and perennials: Both seemed like great investments offering high returns; both were purchased by a large number of people who didn't know much about them; and both left a lot of people wondering what to do with them. After that the comparison goes somewhat awry. Junk bonds were an original creation of the eighties, while perennials were merely being rediscovered by beginners who didn't realize that they had been a mainstay of gardens since the Greeks. And junk bonds had little intrinsic value, while at least a plant is still a plant, although it may not be worth much if you don't know what to do with it.

Until perennials began to fascinate new gardeners in the last twenty years, they had not been widely grown in American gardens for several generations. Interest in perennial flowering plants was a natural next step in the growing gardening enthusiasm that had embraced vegetables and annuals in the sixties and early seventies. More and more people became intrigued with the idea that there were plants out there that not only flowered, but didn't die with the first frost. I was amused by the slogan of one perennial grower, Bluestone Perennials of Mentor, Ohio, whose catalog asked the gardening question of the hour, "Don't you wish your plants came back every year?" and then answered with large type, "PERENNIALS DO!" Suddenly Gertrude Jekyll and William Robinson were being sought out in used bookstores, Hidcote and Sissinghurst became landmarks for horticultural holidays, and Americans began to think that what they really needed was a (or an, depending on your degree of affectation) herbaceous border.

It is hard to know which term causes the most confusion, "perennial" or "border." If you have been growing perennials for the last few years, you have no doubt noticed that perennial is a relative term. With the proper culture and climate, perennials will live longer than annuals. They may live longer than biennials, but after that, it is pretty much a free-for-all. As for the Bluestone question, although we all wish our plants came back every year, and perennials *should,* some do and some don't.

The term "border" is equally problematic. Is there any difference between a bed and a border? The word "bed" still suffers from its Victorian associations with carpet bedding and bedding out, so it is often used to describe a small cultivated area devoted to a temporary display, often of one kind of plant or a group of similar plants. Then you have the workaday bed, the behind-the-scenes catchalls like seed beds or holding beds. Usually any planting area out in the open and visible from all directions, no matter what its contents, is referred to as an island bed. Remember the classic eruptions of cannas or marigolds in the middle of countless American front lawns? That satisfies most definitions of a bed and also shows why many gardeners today try to avoid the term.

Borders by definition run along the edge of something—a wall, a fence, a hedge—or have a definite back. This qualification is often dropped, though, and we are left with the vague sense that a border is bigger than a bed, a more permanent part of the landscape, and filled with a variety of material, of which herbaceous perennials are only one, but by now the most well-known choice.

There are so many common misconceptions about the perennial border that I will list only the obvious: After the initial effort of digging and laying out the border, you will never have to do anything again. Perennials alone will give you a constant succession of bloom from April until frost. Perennials are easier than annuals. A herbaceous border is the best way to use perennials in the landscape.

These misconceptions have developed from a combination of wishful thinking and catalog rhetoric, with a little misreading of William Robinson thrown in to give the justification of history. When Robinson published *The English Flower Garden* in 1883, he was interested in promoting alternatives to the Victorian carpet bedding that was the predominant style of floral ornamentation of the period. So when he states that a border of hardy plants is less work than a display of semitropical annuals that must be changed

The borders of the mind: 1 Agrimony; 2 Symphyandra; 3 Malus; 4 Rheum; 5 Psoralea; 6 Nymphoides; 7 Humulus; 8 Euphorbia; & 9 Lunaria.

three times a year, he is not exactly saying that a herbaceous border is care-free. And although he insists that a border once laid out should be able to stay that way forever, he also makes clear that behind every border there is an equally large reserve bed where perennials are grown until they reach the desired size and shape, and where late-flowering not-quite-perennials like dahlias and even, dare we say it, annuals can be grown along until the proper moment when they are moved into the border to fill any gaps. It is perfectly clear that Robinson is addressing a readership that still had abundant gardening help. It is also clear, both in Robinson's books but even more so in Gertrude Jekyll's, that although a border is an attractive way to use hardy perennials, it is far from being the only or even the best way.

Americans were bitten by the border bug, and it is easy to understand how. From Robinson's engraved illustrations down to the most recent lavish photographs, nothing looks more stunning than a classic perennial border. More important, it is one form of garden art that can be diagrammed, laid out in mass-produced formulas as easy to follow as a paint-by-number set. It requires no imagination, no design experience, and no detailed knowledge of plants, at least until things start to grow wrong. You just stake out your big rectangle, stick in the requisite three stachys or sidalcea or *Sedum* "Autumn Joy" wherever the plan indicates, and in no time you could be right up there between Christopher Lloyd and Beth Chatto.

Most books are cagey about telling us how big a border ought to be, but the Royal Horticultural Society's *Dictionary of Gardening* mentions ominously that "to provide for a succession of blossom from early summer to late autumn a width of fourteen feet will be advisable." That is a *width* of fourteen feet, mind you, which may be only slightly shorter than what you once thought of as your border. As this suggests, the first problem of the classic perennial border is the problem of scale. A width of fourteen feet implies a length of one hundred feet or more, which is what we see at Hidcote or Great Dixter or at the American display gardens that have set out to imitate them. A border of that size managed by a well-trained staff is an astonishing work of art, but few are the backyards that have that kind of space, and fewer still are the gardeners who know what to do with it.

Many enthusiasts and many garden designers convinced themselves and their clients that a kind of compromise could be made by simply making a smaller border. But a small border is a kind of gardening oxymoron, and the reason becomes clear a few years after you plant it. Many perennial favorites are dramatic and effective in two-hundred-foot borders because they get really big. They may start slowly from seed or they may appear demure in their first one-quart containers, and most of them may not look like much in their early years. But just about the time that they start looking like the perennials of your dreams, you realize that they are entirely too big for where you put them, and all around them they have wiped out the choice specimens that you hoped would complete the garden picture.

If you want a small border to work, you must scale down the number of plants you use, which means losing both the sense of wonderful variety perennials can display and the luxuriance of bloom that is the hallmark of the borders we admire most. You must also scale down the size of the plants you use. A seven-foot-tall delphinium is sensational when surrounded by other plants of similar grandeur, but you cannot squeeze more than three or four clumps that size into a bed twenty feet long. American horticulture responded to this need by producing numerous cultivars that don't get enormous, don't sprawl, and don't spread into the next county. You can now create a well-behaved border of a manageable size that has only a few drawbacks: it will not provide that elusive succession of bloom we all seek; it will not be large enough to accommodate the towering showstoppers we admire, but may be too big for small-scale treasures; it may not be the best place to grow more and more of the plants you find you want to grow.

If you jumped on the border bandwagon a decade ago, you may be familiar with these problems. Or you might just keep asking yourself why your border never quite seems to measure up to the pictures in English gardening books. Aside from the scale problems, one reason is that periods of bloom for perennials in America are often much shorter than those in England. Our climate in many areas moves much more rapidly from a short cool spring to a very hot summer. In spite of what all the mail-order catalogs imply, most perennials do not stay in bloom for more than a few weeks, so you do not have the great variety of species all in bloom at the same time that you do in England. Every once in a while we will have a summer like that of 1992 when the weather stayed cool and damp and gray for months and everything stayed in bloom forever. Then you get some inkling of how easy it would be to make the kind of garden pictures that seem to come so effortlessly to the British. But usually we have to contend with a more limited number of species overall, because of our harsh winters or our hot summers or both, and then we have to work within a much more limited time frame for each species. Even if we do manage to achieve a moment of wonderful luxuriance of bloom, it could be over in a week.

Ins and Outs of the Border

WE ALL HAVE friends who are not at their best in a group situation, but whom we love to see one-on-one. Many plants are the same. They may have any one of a variety of personality disorders that makes them unsuitable for the close quarters and communal style of the border, but they still may be plants you would hate to be without. No one in his right mind would try to confine the plume poppy to a border of modest proportions, but wouldn't you miss those oddly shaped glaucous leaves and those towering spires late in August? Anyone who gives border space to *Lysimachia clethroides* will find herself locked in a struggle to the death as the appealing gooseneck appropriates yards of space for its own use. But surely there must be some quiet corner where this shade-tolerant, long-blooming species can rampage at will. There are also statuesque species that are well-behaved enough for border life, but are spectacular when seen apart from the crowd. *Crambe cordifolia* makes an airy explosion of white, four or five feet in any direction—what a shame to jam it in among some pedestrian phlox.

I am amused by William Robinson, who writes the way I garden. All

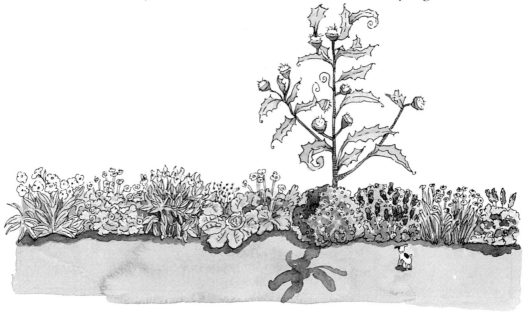

through his chapter on the border he is mentioning plants that would be better *not* grown in the border, just as I am always moving out plants that I think would be better off somewhere else—the Siberian and Japanese iris to the pond side, peonies to line the driveway, asters and rudbeckia out to the pasture. Robinson and I agree about the placement of yuccas, which make spiky exclamation points in the landscape and could make your life miserable as you try to work around them. (Robinson puts them in a bed with red-hot pokers, also spiky, which take up a large amount of space for about three days of bloom.) Little by little I have moved most of the really interesting or absurd plants out of the border, until what are left are the plants that are neither too small nor too big, neither too fussy nor too easy. Little wonder that the borders are the least exciting part of my garden; at times there are more empty holes than plants.

This is the heart of my objection to the border as it is used in perennial gardening today. Perennial and border have become inextricably linked in the public mind, as if the only way that you can enjoy dictamnus or campanulas or amsonia or liatris is to line them up side-by-side in a giant rectangle. Go back to Jekyll and Robinson and you will discover just what a tiny portion of those volumes is concerned with borders as we think of them today. (In my own edition of *The English Flower Garden,* 15 pages of the 956 are devoted to the topic.) Read about the wild garden, the alpine flower garden, the wall garden, spring gardens, the rock garden, the cutting and reserve garden, the hardy fern garden, not to mention summer bedding, and plants in vases and tubs. Read how Miss Jekyll scattered heaths and heathers among the trees on her barren hilltop. See how both these artists stuck in lilies among clusters of shrubs, planted polygonums in distant, "rough" corners with bad soil. Both writers are urging us to use the whole wide world of plants and the full extent of the landscape.

A sunny border will give your primroses sunburn; a shady border will mean no dianthus. A dry border leaves your ligularia limp; a damp one will rot your eremurus. These are cultural quandaries you may face in your efforts to put all your perennials in one border. Stylistic incongruities offer more subtle challenges: can an understated woodlander like vancouveria hold its own against the domineering shades of *Phlox subulata*? Is there a place for the exquisite erythroniums among the jostle of Oriental poppies? A single planting area cannot provide all the growing conditions you need for a wide variety of plants, and it cannot offer the right surroundings for plants that are quiet, or odd, or out of the mainstream. At this stage in your gardening life, the unusual plants might be the ones you most want to grow.

Old-fashioned Beds and New-age Annuals

As you can see in the earlier quotation from the Royal Horticultural Society, somewhere between 1883 and the present the idea developed that the border should offer succession of bloom from early summer to late fall. This is another unfortunate misapprehension that should not be laid at the door of Robinson and Jekyll. Both those writers make it clear that a hardy border is just one of a variety of ways that perennials can be used, and that, although a border should have plants of interest for several seasons, it is not the only place to look for the delights of a particular hour. But that is not the way all too many gardeners today see it. The poor border not only must be all things to all plants, it must be for all seasons as well. If you think that is a questionable proposition in England, imagine what it must mean for a gardener in, say, Texas, where you can expect temperatures in the nineties by mid-April. Those of us in the Northeast who are accustomed to seeing our borders go blank in August can only imagine what it is like to garden in an area where August starts in June and goes on through September.

However difficult it is to maintain constant border bloom in a typical Northeast season of four or five months, it is all but impossible to manage the same with traditional perennials in the South, the Southeast, and California. Yet all these regions have been through their border periods. Nancy Goslee Power, an East Coast–born designer who went west, describes some of the changes she noticed: "I used a lot of perennials when I first came out here; it was what I grew up with and it was what people thought they wanted. But I use them much less now. The client has to understand how they live, has to understand that there is a quiet time, that the plants didn't just die." She now uses a lot more shrubs and big sculptural foliage plants that give a year-round effect. There is a general trend toward those kinds of plants, as well as wider use of native plants, both perennial and annual. Annuals are particularly important in the long seasons of the South and the West. Some plants that we think of as perennials, like primulas, are used as annuals for winter bedding in places where they will not survive the hot summers.

The obvious way to deal with succession of bloom in almost any climate is to salt your so-called perennial planting with annuals and don't think all those National Trust gardens are above such tactics. Haven't you wondered, too, about the presence of much-photographed biennials such as digitalis and verbascum, both mainstays of mixed borders? Both species are mostly biennial and spend their first quiet year sequestered in a propagation range, waiting to be moved into the limelight when needed. (Foxgloves are so accommodating that they can be moved while in bloom to any space that needs a filler when a photographer or a garden tour is coming.) Once again, these tactics are much easier if you have a two-hundred-foot border, a reserve bed in which to grow the annuals or biennials until their moment of glory, and a gardener to plop them in when you are ready. Otherwise you end up shoehorning in a few timid seedlings, which hang on for about a week until the perennials around them burst forth and reclaim the space.

When perennials were at peak trendiness in the eighties, it was fashionable to deride the annuals of yesteryear and to look back at the petunias of our past as some kind of adolescent folly. Now, there are some annuals I would be only too happy never to see again—chrome yellow marigolds, pale pink begonias with leaves like the finest plastic, New Guinea impatiens, which brought all the worst shades of that useful deep-shade bloomer out into the screaming sunlight. But the word *annual* is just as vague a term for a huge class of plants as *perennial*. There are wonderful annuals, just as there are awful ones, and no gardener can afford to write off this invaluable group of flowers.

Why should annuals vs. perennials be an either/or proposition? It is rather like refusing to eat chicken because you also like fish. As we discussed earlier when we spoke of habits of growth, it is difficult even to be very sure of our terms when we speak of some plants as one-year propositions and some as permanent residents. *Salvia gregii* is a shrubby perennial in Texas or California; I can use it as an annual up north if I start plants early. And it is impossible to make inane generalizations like: perennials are easier (or harder) than annuals; perennials are more beautiful than annuals; perennials are more rewarding or more challenging than annuals; real gardeners don't bother with annuals. Annuals are simply different from perennials, and you are cheating yourself and your garden if you confine your interest to one or the other.

There is no question that it is not easy to grow annuals and perennials in the same border unless you have a lot of space and a lot of time. In many display gardens, big areas in a border are planted with early bloomers like tulips, which are then lifted, discarded, and replaced with annuals for later bloom. For a home gardener with moderate space, it is much easier simply to have some small beds set aside for that kind of changing display. The use of alternative beds of this kind has many advantages. It makes it possible to bring flowers to parts of the garden other than the border. It means that annuals don't have to wage war for bed space with larger, stronger perennials, a war the annuals usually lose unless you constantly referee. A small bed of anything as appetizing as tulips can be more easily defended against rabbits or deer—you can avoid having a fortress of chicken wire around your entire border. A separate bed makes it possible to have a planting of one kind of flower, which is exciting and different from the mixed floral effects of the border. Some bulbs, like tulips, are particularly striking by themselves. (It is also convenient to have a few empty beds that can be completely dug up, filled with fresh compost, and planted all at once in the fall with new bulbs.) Early, cool-weather biennials like wallflowers can be set out in the fall for spring bloom, then replaced with later annuals or summer bulbs. Alternative beds mean that you can plant out chrysanthemums somewhere other than center stage in your border, where they will sit motionless until late September.

There has been a growing interest in out-of-the-ordinary annuals, which makes it possible to fill those beds with more than striped petunias. How about a six-foot-tall explosion of bright orange tithonia, or the huge sticky rosettes of *Nicotiana sylvestris,* sporting spires of fragrant, droopy white blossom? There are spectacular salvias that erase the stigma of the formerly ubiquitous *Salvia splendens. Salvia coccinea* is a showstopping rich scarlet, which starts late, then looks better and better when all else is looking worse until hard frost. The long, trailing pink strands of love-lies-bleeding, worth growing for the name alone; satiny red flax; chalk-white, ground-hugging

Zinnia acerosa; the extravagant butterflys of schizanthus—what adventure is available for the price of a packet of seed! True, there is a risk that some varieties won't work well for you—that godetia may need a season longer or shorter than your own, that clarkia may just be too homesick for the Rockies to produce in New Jersey, even for a season—but then you simply have a bed ready to clear out for those late chrysanthemums. If you have several spots for experiments each year, one or two failures will not amount to much. It is fun to change completely the character of the plantings from year to year—a low, vivid carpet of mixed annual phlox can next become a mass of mallows; sprawling cosmos can give way to a fussy, fragrant Victorian posy of heliotrope.

Going beyond the Gladiolus

WHILE WE ARE rediscovering the delights of annuals, let us explore the subject of summer bulbs. It is unfortunate that the dominant image that phrase conjures up is usually a funereal spray of multicolored gladiolus. Or the volcano of cannas on the front lawn. Or the flapping, blotched, streaked, and striped tissue of caladiums. All these are summer bulbs, I have to admit, and it is easy to see why many gardeners decide not to pursue the topic. But there are less overbearing, less overworked bulb species that can be delightful for a season and can sometimes surprise us by coming back for more.

Crocosmias and montebretias might be better known if the catalogs and the nomenclature authorities could agree on exactly which is which. According to *Hortus,* they are crocosmia botanically, except for the ones that are tritonia, and mostly called montebretia popularly. Generally speaking, the big ones are crocosmia and the small ones tritonia. Whatever they are, they are shades of orange-gold or deep, wonderful red in the cultivar "Lucifer," airy wands of color from one foot to three feet in height, blooming in August or September from the previous spring's planting. They are cheap, widely available, and almost foolproof unless you mistake the early foliage for grass and pull them up, as I have on many occasions. The bulbs are so small and the foliage so narrow that I often stick them in open spots of a border—they need less room and less attention than most annuals. Best of all, they frequently turn out to be much hardier than predicted. I have clumps that have been coming back in Zone 4 for five or six years in places with good drainage—always the key to success with bulbs. Even if they last for only a season they are worth the very small effort.

Flamboyant, top-heavy florist favorites may have made you gladiolus shy, and that is understandable—those fleshy, awkward products of manipulative hybridizing never look real coming out of the ground. It is a shame, too, since they are so cheap and easy. If we go back to some of the *Ur*-glads, however, we might find some pretty plants. *Gladiolus byzantinus* is a cottage garden favorite all through the South and West, but it can be grown much farther north than many gardeners suspect. It might be accused of being magenta, but a clear, vivid shade, and it holds its three-foot spears upright. *Gladiolus x colvillei* is an old garden hybrid with all the charm of a species bulb. This is frequently advertised as "the hardy gladiolus" and it sometimes is, with good drainage. But even if it isn't, it is a lovely addition to the August scene, with its graceful spikes of white or peach or rose orchidlike blooms. An exotic touch for a reasonable price.

Acidantheras were gladiolus once, at least to the authorities, but they always had a distinctive charm and now they have a genus of their own. These have been unequivocal about not surviving Zone 4 winters, but you can either lift and replant them or simply buy new ones each year—hardly an extravagance at about fifty cents a bulb. They make an arching fountain of slowly opening white blossoms marked with deep purple that lasts for weeks.

These are just a few of the most available summer bulbs and they are my favorites, but you don't have to stop here. Go on to *Ornithogalum thyrsoides* (popularly called "chincherinchee," as if that makes it any easier)—these icy-white wands of stars have the unusual drawback of flowering for so long that they don't look real. Homeria occasionally pops up with peach or copper funnel-shaped flowers, but is not perfectly reliable for me. It is glorious in California, like so many things. Ixia are ethereal to the point of invisibility, but you will find them charming if you can find them at all.

It is hard to exaggerate the value of these plants in the late-summer garden. We have all experienced that depressing moment in August when the only things in bloom seem to be some form of yellow composite. I have nothing against either the color or the family, and in Zone 4 we can't always afford to be choosy, but we all want to have a few alternatives. Bulb plants offer completely different flower and leaf forms as well as colors that either harmonize with your late perennials, like the crocosmias, or go off in another direction. Best of all, they are plants that are growing and coming into bloom at a time when other flowers have either stopped blooming or have been blooming for so long that you almost wish they would stop. Summer bulbs add that invaluable element to the garden—something to look forward to.

You might keep in mind that even some hardy bulbs can be planted in spring for late-summer bloom. If you have trouble with late frosts, for example, and find it difficult to grow certain lilies, you can plant them in April and have them bloom in August or September. Lilies are too expensive for most of us to consider as disposable annuals, but it is worthwhile planting even a few each spring to guarantee some lilies late in the year. If you didn't get around to putting in your allium in the fall, some of the late-summer species will be fine after spring planting.

After a few years of experimentation you will know with greater accuracy how long it takes certain bulbs to flower in your garden. Then you can manipulate the timing of your planting to bring species to flower when you need them most. You can also prolong their blooming period by starting some bulbs early, others a few weeks later if you have an extended fall season. Once the gladiolus and crocosmia prove hardy for you, you will no longer be able to control their schedule this way, so you may still want to get some new bulbs each year.

Perennial vs. Permanent

IT IS DISAPPOINTING, to say the least, when we find that the so-called perennials in which we invested turn out to be a great deal less than perennial in our gardens. You can hardly open a book on perennials without seeing the seven-foot spires of delphinium dominating a border, so why do they make a quick exit when you try to grow them? Why would the vibrant Maltese cross be stunning one year and missing the next? You may keep aquilegia from one year to the next, but it never comes up in the same place twice and it is always a different color.

It takes several years of gardening with perennials to discover which plants are indeed long-term residents and which are transients. Your particular climate, exposure, soil, and degree of attentiveness will all play a part in the longevity of any one species. More important, you will discover that it really doesn't matter if all your plants don't behave like peonies and bloom for a hundred years. "Oh, that never stays long for me," is an oft-repeated refrain in conversation with experienced growers, and it is seldom a cause for anguish. If you like a plant and want to grow it, you can always have a few new ones coming along to replace your favorite when it goes.

The discovery of individual plant mortality is nothing to the news that the perennial border as a whole isn't permanent, either. Every seven to ten years the entire planting should be dug up and renewed. This is a crushing announcement to anyone who was counting on the border to be a thing of beauty that was a joy forever, preferably with as little interference as possible. But if you have been working on your border for the last decade, you have probably had some inkling that an overhaul was due. The most important reason is for soil conditioning. Even if you have been fertilizing and top dressing, mulching and manuring, your soil will still need renewal all the way down to two or three feet, and the only way to do that is to dig everything out. We will have a much more thorough discussion of soil management later; for now, just try to absorb the idea that all this is ahead of you. Besides the need to renew the soil, a complete overhaul will give you the chance to divide those plants you haven't quite gotten around to dividing, an opportunity to clear out weeds and grasses that have become more permanent residents than many of your perennials, and the chance to straighten out some of the more implausible of your planting combinations.

It is astonishing how few books on perennials will tell you straight out that this kind of major renovation is necessary; perhaps if they did we would not have the infatuation with borders from which American gardening is only now recovering. I won't try to tell you that this is not a huge amount of work, but it doesn't all have to be done at once, and it is exciting when you finish to be back at that stage when, however briefly, your border again resembles the paint-by-number plans you may once have followed. Many gardeners find it easiest to do half a border in one season, half in the next. This decision may depend on the size of the border and how much help you can muster, but you should do it in big chunks, at least fifteen feet at a time, because you will need a lot of room to handle the soil effectively without stomping on the existing plants. Spread a tarp to collect soil and plants; keep plants in big clumps until you are ready to replace them, then divide them before you replant. I find that most big, tough perennials are fine for several days out of the ground if they are out of direct sun and kept moist; in fact, I have tried occasionally to reduce the number of excess asters or phlox or *Campanula persicifolia* by leaving them exposed for weeks, only to be driven to guilty replanting when I notice that they are still growing and even flowering in big bare-root clumps. More delicate species can be wrapped in damp newspaper and plastic bags.

There are a number of big, hardy, long-lived perennials that can be used in a border that does not require frequent intervention and redigging: peonies, Oriental poppies, Siberian iris, New England asters, some of the hardy geraniums. Each climate zone will have a list of stalwarts that will flourish under almost any conditions. And there are a few high-risk species that cannot be dug up without great danger: dictamnus, baptisia, eremurus, anything with a long single taproot. A border of these sturdy and/or intransigent individuals could be lovely in some seasons and would certainly require less attention than the borders we see diagrammed in oh-so-many books. Yearly top dressing will probably be enough for these plants in most soils. But is this the only border you want? Once you try to combine these heavy hitters with a variety of less vigorous species, you run into all the old border disputes. You cannot expect the more delicate penstemons to keep pace with the prodigal peonies; how do you keep a little creeping veronica from being crushed by waves of gypsophila? If you want your border to exhibit many different kinds of plants, you should anticipate redigging and replanting on a regular schedule, if only to maintain a balance of power. If you include a few irresistible immovables in your border you will have to work around them. Keep in mind that many of these big shrublike species, such as the peonies and asters mentioned above, don't need border coddling.

They will do happily in low-maintenance parts of the garden where they won't be threatening flowers that can't fight back.

Books will go into great detail about when certain plants can be divided successfully, but as we found with moving trees and shrubs the best time is when you have time, regardless of season. I like to do it in August, when things look wretched anyway—it gives at least one part of the garden a kind of springlike freshness. If you do it in spring, you may lose some early summer bloom, but you can stick in lots of annuals to carry you through at least one season until the perennials fight back. If you do it in fall, you can put in lots of bulbs for the following spring.

Breaking up the Border

THE BORDER WAS never meant to be an all-or-nothing monopoly, the beginning and end of flowers in a garden. Maturing American gardeners are realizing this as they gradually recover from their fatal attraction to all things English. If you have had success with your border, there is clearly no reason to change, but you might consider ways of using some of your perennials in other parts of the property. We spoke earlier about a few alternatives: naturalizing, underplanting, overplanting. Think of places that could be developed for native plants of your particular region in meadow or woodland plantings. Consider combining shrubs, bulbs, and perennials in informal arrangements around the house. Try perennials or annuals in containers that can highlight patios or porches. Your border experiences have introduced you to many plants: now find better ways to use them across the entire landscape.

Our gardens become more personal and more original as we work on them over the years. We become less and less concerned with clichéd ideas of what a garden ought to be, and more and more interested in what our particular garden can be. It may be that a border is just the thing for your situation and range of interests. But it is more likely that the border is there because when you first thought of growing perennials that seemed like the only possibility. It still is a possibility, but it should not be the only one. What happens when you decide to grow fourteen species of verbascum or begin to amass the largest collection of drabas ever seen in Nebraska? Where are you going to put all your hardy cactus? (Wouldn't a fine cluster of verbascum be a wonderful way to accent your mailbox? How about a clump of those cactus on the spot where your neighbor's dog comes through the fence?) As we grow as gardeners, these are the byways of horticulture that lure us in unexpected directions; these are the plants that give our gardens personality. These are not plants that belong in the traditional border, so the border must change to meet our needs and our expanding range of interests. You can have perennials within borders or without. You can have beds without perennials or with them. You can have a garden with borders, but don't let the border mark the limit of your gardening horizon.

7

How Green Was

My Valley

. . . .

Anyone WHO WITNESSED the return to gardening that took place from the mid-sixties through the seventies would be inclined to see a connection between gardening and environmental concern. In the Age of Aquarius we were going back to the land, discovering the richness of nature, eschewing the poisoned fruits of commerce, and growing our own organic everything. What could be more ecologically correct than gardening?

A quick glance at the pesticide shelves of any garden center can provide a sobering answer to that question. The average suburban gardener has access to an arsenal of poisons that would make Lucretia Borgia green. And this has been the case for at least the last hundred years. Horticulture in the nineteenth century reeked of nicotine and lead arsenate; bichloride of mercury, when not starring in detective novels, had a prominent place in potting sheds and greenhouses. As we move into this century, starting in the forties, DDT once hung in the air like a mushroom cloud. This was the new panacea, proclaimed as the outdoor equivalent of penicillin, although it had much more in common with the atomic bomb being developed at the same time. Like nuclear weapons, DDT guaranteed the prompt, decisive removal of anything that moved, and it was only after many years that the fallout effect could be gauged. Enlightened by hindsight, we shudder to read in not-so-old gardening texts prescriptions of DDT against anything from ants to thrips, and we congratulate ourselves that such things couldn't happen today. But can we really be sure? If we read the fine print on a package of Sevin, for example, we discover that this widely used, supposedly "safe" insecticide is highly toxic to bees and should not be used in a situation where it could enter the water supply. The label leaves to our imagination the possible damage that could be caused to fish and other wildlife, but what gardener would not be appalled to think of injuring the honeybee? Yet production of Sevin for sale worldwide is about twenty-five million pounds a year.

Most of us may not have had a specific environmental agenda when we started to garden, and that is probably just as well. In these days of ever-increasing ecological complexity, even making a garden might be considered environmentally unsound. We like to think we are improving the world by planting trees and flowers and fertilizing the soil, but one could also argue that what we are doing is introducing invasive foreign species, depleting mineral resources, interrupting natural plant successions, and otherwise un-balancing the ecology of an area. Now, it is unlikely that the plot of land we undertook to cultivate was anything like a natural habitat to begin with, but that is hardly an excuse to write off completely our environmental responsibility. For many of us, gardening was an introduction to other forms of life, and it is to be hoped that in the ten years or so that we have been doing this, we have learned something of the beauty and complexity of the nonhuman world and realized that Homo sapiens has to make every effort to respect other species on this planet.

The War of the Worlds

IF YOU DIDN'T spend much time outdoors before you began to garden, you probably never gave the insect world much thought. Most of us abhor roaches and resent mosquitoes, admire honeybees, delight in butterflies, and avoid wasps and spiders whenever possible. All the rest of those six- or eight-legged creatures, as well as some with no legs at all, were pretty much lumped together in our minds as "bugs" and dismissed as being beneath our notice.

This attitude undergoes dramatic revision when you start to garden. For a couple of years you might get off easily—a few spotted leaves, a few twisted buds or nibbled petals. But as the garden becomes established, so do the populations that call it supper. After investing heavily in roses you suddenly have bushes that shimmer with the iridescent green and bronze of Japanese beetles. Your primulas have summoned slugs by the shovelful; caterpillars adorn your trees with tent cities. Sooner or later you declare war.

The available arsenal has improved to the point where a constant cycle of spraying will kill some of the insects some of the time. This rather dubious

success must be weighed against the negative factors: spraying is, in itself, a very unpleasant business; you are exposing yourself and your family to possibly dangerous chemicals; you are eliminating a great number of harmless or potentially beneficial insects; you may be harming birds, reptiles, fish, or mammals. It is ironic that some of us might eagerly sign petitions demanding the rescue of seals, whales, or wolves, yet think nothing of grabbing the nearest aerosol to wipe out an inconvenient insect. Even if the crop you were saving were financially important or necessary for the survival of your family, it would still be hard to decide that pesticides are worth it. And most of us are not gardening for survival. When you consider that gardening is supposed to be a pleasure, a recreation, and that the result is supposed to increase the beauty around us, it seems absurd to spend time engaged in chemical warfare against a foe that will always have other ranks to send into battle. Is it really worth fighting to the death for a dahlia?

It may be hard to believe, but many of the gardeners who are most lavish in their application of pesticides are those who grow their own fruits and vegetables. Surely one of the major reasons for vegetable gardening is to

125

produce food untouched by the poisons used by commercial agriculture. But vegetable gardening is product-oriented. Only a few of us are eccentric enough to grow corn or broccoli for their decorative effect alone, and people who sow and hoe spinach feel they are entitled to bring their rewards to the table. They don't expect a plague of barely visible crawling creatures to stand in their way.

Because most vegetables are annuals, the effects of insects can be more devastating because it is much more of an all-or-nothing proposition: One week of root maggot and you can say good-bye to cabbage for the rest of the summer. A common rationalization for the use of insecticides in the home garden is the argument that all store-bought produce has been exposed to chemicals, so it is not going to make much difference if we use them ourselves. Although it's true that you might be ingesting small amounts of pesticide from the food you buy, at least you are not spraying it around your own property, mixing it in your sink, spilling it down your pants, handling the residue every time you weed or cultivate. You are not inadvertently spraying it on the lettuce your children love to nibble straight from the bed.

I may sound unduly harsh here, and it might well be that anyone who would read this chapter has long ago hung up his spray guns. But I occasionally host a radio talk show on gardening that takes phone calls from all over the country and I would guess that eighty percent of the calls are from people who want to wipe out some portion of the insect population. One year on Earth Day I delivered a little homily about the dangers of pesticides and immediately took a call from a man who wanted to rid his house and garden of the hundreds of ladybugs that had taken up residence. I have heard from people who hate earthworms, people who fight centipedes and ground beetles, all beneficial creatures. What is one to do?

For people who feel they must spray, there are now more products on the market that discourage bugs and steer them toward your neighbors rather than killing them. There are numerous soap preparations that cleverly mimic the effect achieved by the cottage gardener who throws her dishwater out the back door over her flowers, a regimen of pest control now recognized for its true value. There are more specific poisons that eliminate only one enemy at a time—the use of which, however, demands that you know a Diabrotica beetle from a chinch bug. There are more biological controls available, either bugs that eat other bugs, or bacterial diseases like milky spore that incapacitate the bad guys.

There are also more products that proclaim loudly that they are "all natural," as if this in itself were a guarantee of their safety. Find out before you use them exactly what that means. Keep in mind that many of the world's most deadly poisons are indeed all natural—amanita mushrooms, snake venom, atropine, digitalis, curare. As Lucretia Borgia undoubtedly knew, "all natural" has never meant that something won't kill you.

One time-honored environmentally sound preventative is handpicking, particularly against big enemies such as caterpillars and Japanese beetles. This can be a healthy outlet for the kind of child that pulls the wings off flies. In fact, many young children enjoy climbing into the cherry trees to rip out the cotton-candy fluff of the tent caterpillars. It is even better if you can find the egg cases of these moths during the winter, subtle little lumps of hard brown bubbles around the twigs of fruit trees. Children are especially clever at spotting these and scraping them off. This activity may sound tedious, but it is actually a pleasant excuse to wander through the snowy landscape and feel that you are doing something constructive. Watching your plants carefully is the first step toward controlling insect damage.

Physical insect deterrents, like paper or tin-can collars around young vegetables, are an old-time method that has not been outdated; circles of tar paper on the ground around your cabbages could do the trick against those root maggots. Modern technology has produced new materials, such as polypropylene seed blankets, which speed germination and early growth of lawn grass and annuals while protecting them from depredation in the crucial first weeks. Chasing white and yellow cabbage butterflies with a net is a delightful way for the family to spend a summer afternoon and it could reduce the number of caterpillars that attack all members of the mustard family.

Good plant health is crucial to any program of pest control, or to no pest control. If a plant is in good condition, it will usually survive even a serious infestation. Overall garden hygiene is equally important, since piles of debris provide breeding places for unwanted insects, and lack of air circulation contributes greatly to the growth of funguses.

Insects can be as interesting and beautiful as your flowers. Because the two are so closely connected, you gain a great deal by enjoying your bugs rather than fighting them. For example, if you grow hops, after a few years you will meet the caterpillar that is making holes in the leaves of your plants. This may be annoying, but it is rarely fatal, and to offset the injury you are able to enjoy the Hop Merchant, one of the beautiful fritillary butterflies. That frightful, spectacular striped-and-spotted caterpillar the size of your finger may do damage to your parsley, but how much parsley do you really need? Sacrifice a few stalks for the presence of the black swallowtail. Morning glories, bindweed, and other convolvulus relatives could introduce you to the gold bug, a sparkling hymenoptera flashy enough to star in Poe's story.

Too often we don't realize how much we enjoy this kind of activity until it is gone. In the last few years there was a virus attacking honeybee populations in our area, and my next-door neighbor had to destroy her hives. The garden was desolate—a whole layer of life was gone. It wasn't just the silence and the loss of all that pleasant bustle. Flowers were not fertilized, fruit and vegetables failed to form, seeds never showed. This year Diane started her hives again and the entire neighborhood rejoiced. Once again the thyme was a humming carpet, and the linden gave out a buzz that could be heard down the street. I would be willing to give up a lot of plants before I would use a product that might endanger this crucial element of the garden.

As we discussed earlier, plant selection is the best defense against the worst insect and disease problems. You may not know which plants are the most susceptible when you buy them, but once you discover that certain species can be kept alive only by a steady regimen of spray, get rid of them. There are too many plants out there that you may never get to try—the bugs will make it easier for you to move on to something new and exciting. Increased variety of species is another way to outwit the enemy. No matter if this is the day of the locust or the year of the earwig, there will always be some plants having a great season.

One of the most valuable lessons a garden has to offer is an awareness of the cycles of nature. Each growing season has a different character, shaped by weather and time and circumstances we know nothing about until we see their effects upon the growing things around us. Each year has its paramount pest and its own personal combination of temperature and wind and precipitation. Each element can guarantee that this year will not be like any other, in the garden and out of it. Last year was cool and damp; we ate chanterelles every day for two months and slugs ate everything else. This year it is hot and dry; the tomatoes are thriving and so is every form of caterpillar known to horticulture. Last year the hollyhocks were covered with rust on the bottom and aphids on the top; this year they are inexplicably immaculate, without any chemical intervention. One year the Chinese lanterns are eaten to the ground by beetles; the next they are back and three feet tall. I could labor to explain some of that; I could labor even more to prevent some of it. But what difference does it make in the long run? When you have only a dozen tiny plants, every pest seems prodigious, every disease seems desperate. Ten years of gardening and hundreds of plants give you some perspective on these cycles—a few more years may make you genuinely interested in them.

Clearing out Environmental Clutter

THE PESTICIDE PROBLEM is an easy one to remedy, since all it requires is that we do nothing. For a while we may experience a knee-jerk reaction whenever we spot a slug, but soon we hardly notice them. What we mostly notice is that we don't spend several hours a week wearing a twenty-gallon backpack sprayer and a gas mask. But there are other areas of gardening ecology that might take more effort and thought.

For centuries, the nonplant materials of gardening were both biodegradable and endlessly recycled: clay pots, wooden flats, peach baskets, burlap bags, cotton string. Plastic changed all that as it changed the way that people bought plants. Plastic pots made it possible to grow and market plants in a completely different way. The pots are extremely cheap and lightweight and almost indestructible, making it much easier to grow and ship plants in containers. But the result is visible in garages and toolsheds across

America—a mountain of green and black plastic, and most of it of a kind that cannot be recycled. Although the pots can be reused indefinitely, I know few gardeners who are potting up at the same rate that they are acquiring plants, so there is always an uneven balance of trade.

This may seem like a petty concern, but many environmental problems are caused by petty concerns multiplied by a population of billions. Reuse your pots, return them to local nurseries for their reuse, buy peat pots whenever possible, and encourage their use by your suppliers. Reuse paper cups for your seedlings. Urge nurseries to sell plants bare root in early spring. This used to be the standard way of offering a wide variety of trees and shrubs for sale, and it has almost been done away with because of container packaging. It is still the most economical way to obtain many young plants. Encourage local growers to sell field-grown perennials by digging them to order and wrapping them in damp newspaper. Only small operations can work this way efficiently, but these are often the places that sell the best and most interesting plants. True, you have to plant them when you get home instead of letting them sit around in their pots for two months. Both your backyard and your plants might benefit from that kind of discipline.

Frugality has always been a hallmark of horticulture; gardeners were reusing and recycling long before those terms became slogans of the environmental movement. We shouldn't let the *nouveau riche* habits of the affluent eighties change that. There are many more supposedly labor-saving gadgets available to gardeners now than there were twenty or thirty years ago, but how many of them are tools that we really need? Are the foul fumes and raucous noise of a leaf blower a necessary replacement for the quiet scratch of a bamboo rake? Isn't an electric edger something you can live without? Don't you find that you have accumulated a variety of plastic gardening objects that would be better made of wood or metal, as they were for centuries: stakes, trellises, labels, watering cans? It may cost more these days to be environmentally frugal, but the rewards will be evident in our toolsheds, in our air quality, in our landfills.

....

Habits and Habitats

IT IS MORE than likely that your property was not an untouched natural habitat even before you arrived there. If you are living in a house on the land, you may consider that the area has already undergone more serious rearrangement than you will cause by planting a few flowers. But what if you are gardening in a sensitive ecological zone? What if you are, even without knowing it, living in a unique natural situation that might require a very different approach than the usual combination of lawn, trees, and shrubs? What if you are perched on the edge of a pine barren, or halfway up some towering western mountain? What if your property was once part of the great central grasslands, the Midwestern oak savannas, the arid plains, or the desert? Perhaps you are beginning to realize that the landscaping clichés of the American Northeast are inappropriate, time-consuming, and environmentally wrong for numerous areas of the United States. You may have spent the last ten years working in defiance of the climate, soil, and landscape that surrounds you. This realization should not be cause for chagrin. It may take more effort and imagination to change the direction of your garden, but once you are working with the environment instead of against it, you will find that you have a much more original garden as well as one that is less wasteful of our natural resources.

Laurie Otto, of Milwaukee, Wisconsin, offers a perfect case study of an environmental awakening. Miss Otto, who is now well into her seventies, has been called the grand dame of natural landscaping; she has been honored by the Garden Clubs of America for conservation education. But back in the sixties she was simply another homeowner in the suburbs of the Midwest, with a small, pleasant house surrounded by an acre of lawn and one-hundred-foot-tall Norway spruces. On the first Earth Day, in 1970, she attended a lecture on prairie plants that brought back memories of her childhood: rudbeckia, purple coneflowers, goldenrod, asters, liatris. "I thought: My God, I've got a whole acre of lawn—I don't need all that lawn!" That thought was the start of a completely new direction for her property. When she bought the lot forty years before, there were "all these adorable baby spruces—sixty-seven of them. I took out a few during the first energy crises just to get some light." More were felled as she began to turn her lawn back into the prairie that had once been there. "At first I'd just make a hole in the grass and stick in some of those prairie plants. Now we see more clearly the importance of plant communities and the way the native grasses and forbs work together."

Laurie Otto's concern for the environment and her ever-wilder garden grew together, and she began helping others who were interested in what she was doing—first in her own community, then farther afield. Of course, not everyone shared her viewpoint, especially back in the seventies. "Oh, I have one neighbor who still won't speak to me after I took out those trees. Just because a plant is one hundred feet tall doesn't mean it can't be a weed, and Norway spruces are weeds." She has had to battle "weed commissioners," town officials whose lives are dedicated to making sure the American suburbs continue to be a well-watered wasteland of lawns. But because of her efforts and the efforts of others with a similar outlook, prairie gardening is now a widespread trend throughout the Midwest. There are numerous nurseries providing plants specific to this region that will flourish in a natural setting.

You may not be ready for a complete conversion to this kind of eco-awareness, but you might consider gradually changing parts of your property to something more in sympathy with your surroundings, especially if you have extensive areas of lawn that require watering and chemical fertilizer. A lot of this is just common sense: If you live in a natural woodland, learn about woodland plants instead of struggling with roses. If your house is on the beach you have a particularly fragile environment on your doorstep and should do everything to protect it. Much of America west of the Mississippi could use new approaches to the landscape, like Laurie Otto's, which reduce water use and take advantage of unique native plants. You don't have to forsake roses completely, or even cut down all your Norway spruces. But let some of your landscape display the natural heritage every part of America has to offer. You will learn more about the landscape around you, and you will be able to share the beauties of that landscape with others.

....

Where Did the Water Go?

THE RECENT DROUGHT in California brought reduced water use into temporary vogue, but one winter's showers were enough to submerge most drought anxieties. People are only too eager to believe that drought is a temporary inconvenience, in spite of universal evidence to the contrary. California is a desert state, as are many of the states of the West. Water can make these places into the Garden of Eden, but water is not an infinitely expandable resource, and each new housing development, each new condo complex, further stretches a system that is already overextended.

Several years of drought brought dramatic changes to the landscape industry as a whole new world of plants became popular and a new vocabulary of gardening entered the vernacular: Xeriscape, point irrigation, drip system. Garden designers began to unveil bold and beautiful strategies for bringing flowers out of the dust. Although the drought years were difficult for both commercial agriculture and backyard gardening, it was an exciting time, as more and more homeowners abandoned azaleas and bluegrass in favor of plants like abronia, phacelia, sphaeralcea, chilopsis, or cercidium.

The territory gained in the past six years could be lost to lawns overnight, however, if everyone decides the worst is over. It may seem unfair to indict California for this attitude when vast portions of the western U.S. suffer from the same problems. But trends spring up and flower on the coast. When California suffered its water woes, half the continent turned off the sprinklers. Reduced water use became a rallying cry in New York, Chicago, and Dallas, not just in L.A. We cannot afford to lose ground now that the water pressure is on and the environmental pressure is off. Reconstruct areas of your garden now to prepare for water restrictions in the future—there are many parts of this country that may expect restrictions to be the norm by the next century. Here are a few of the most basic changes you should consider:

· *Cut back on lawn areas.*
· *Increase use of mulches, especially around trees and shrubs.*
· *Install point-specific watering systems and monitor them carefully.*

133

> • *Organize beds of flowers and shrubs according to water needs, so that only a few areas need extra water.*
> • *Become familiar with drought-resistant plants, both natives and species from other arid parts of the world.*

A garden that is developed or reconstructed on a lean water ration today will be ready for shortages tomorrow. During the California drought we learned to resent the emerald acres that had once defined our vision of paradise. We began to be excited by new kinds of beauty, by new surface textures and leaf outlines and tones that were silver and tawny rather than lime. Garden designers responded to the challenges of that time with a flood of ideas that are only beginning to enrich the larger world of horticulture. Let's not lose this breadth of vision when there are puddles in the street and reflections in the reservoirs.

Wildflower Ethics

THE SUBJECT OF wildflowers keeps surfacing. Wildflower gardening has been growing as a trend in America throughout the last century and especially in the last twenty years. The woodland wildflower garden, primarily an American invention, is now well established in many gardening cultures, and is frequently embellished with species from the woodlands of China and Japan. Today's current fad for meadow gardening has brought America's field flowers into the backyard. Rock garden enthusiasts have made us aware of the treasures of the mountaintops. All this has enriched the selection of plants we can grow in our gardens and enhanced our appreciation of these lovely species in the wild. But the popularity of our natives has brought with it other environmental dilemmas.

Where did you get the plants with which to start your wildflower collection? Did you grow them from seed, or purchase them from a reputable nursery that grew them from seeds or cuttings? Or did you perhaps go out and gather a few plants ("No one will ever notice") from the state park up the road, or from that woodland acreage no one seems to own? Perhaps you tried that mail-order outfit that offered such bargain prices—too bad the plants you received were mostly D.O.A.

It should be unnecessary to say that taking plants from the wild is immoral and usually illegal. It is also often pointless, because even if you succeed in moving plants successfully (a very big "if"), you may not keep them alive for long. Many woodland beauties such as trillium have an extremely long single root that snakes its way through rocky soil and snaps off dishearteningly just when you think you have it all. Some have such specific requirements for light, soil, and water that it is risky to transplant them even from one part of your yard to another. Unless you are extremely adept in all areas of cultivation, your losses will far outnumber your gains.

Many of our most beautiful natives are slow to germinate and slow to grow, which is why few general-interest nurseries make a business of selling them. When you see trillium, cypripedium, and bloodroot offered at reasonable or bargain rates, particularly in mail-order catalogs, you can at least suspect that the plants you are buying were not propagated but torn up from the wild. If you have had any experience in growing these plants yourself, you should realize that the chances are extremely low that frail woodland species will survive commercial harvesting techniques and the indignities of the U.S. post office. Besides the disappointment of buying something that dies, you should feel guilty for paying unscrupulous sellers to wipe out wild populations of some of our choice and possibly endangered native plants.

Beginning gardeners are easy dupes of plant exploiters. When you first start, you don't realize how long it takes to produce a trillium of saleable size or understand what is involved in germinating orchids or the spores of rare ferns. Many of us don't know which plants are rare and which are not. Ignorance is no excuse, as the law recognizes. But now we are older and wiser gardeners: we should be responsible in procuring our plant treasures; we should encourage laws that protect wild plants in every part of the world. Right? Unfortunately, none of that is true; age and experience only contribute to other forms of plant abuse.

The passionate plantsman, the consummate collector can be a far more vicious destroyer of rare plants than the blundering beginner. A neophyte

might dig up clumps of lythrum along the highway; although this is stupid and illegal, it will result in greater harm to his garden than to the environment. But only a knowledgeable and unscrupulous collector would climb the Sierras in search of *Primula suffrutescens* and pull it out of the ground. At horticulture clubs and plant societies you can hear the same justifications: "Only I will be able to grow and propagate it." "It would only get eaten by some sheep if I left it there." "I'm going to share it with others." "There were loads of them up there; no one will miss just one." All this is intended to disguise the most basic urge of the collector, which is to have what no one else can possess.

Besides unlawfully collecting native plants in this country, such collectors also contribute to the depredation of rare species in other countries by ordering plants and bulbs that have been wild collected. Few gardeners just starting out are going to scour the catalogs in search of some *Sternbergia candida* to grow—exotics like those can only find buyers among knowledgeable plantsmen with uncertain ethics. Bulb harvesting in the wild is an important part of the economy of many underdeveloped countries such as Turkey, which ships tons of bulbs each season and which is rapidly eliminating many native bulb species in the wild.

Conservation groups have pressured the major bulb sellers here and abroad to state in their catalogs whether a species is cultivated or harvested in the wild. A great many beautiful once-wild species are now grown commercially and can be purchased without guilt. Check your catalogs and resist those bargain snowdrops from the Caucasus. Don't hesitate to ask your suppliers about the origin of their bulbs. Make it clear that this is a matter of importance to you so that it will become a matter of importance to them.

There are more and more specialized nurseries that propagate and sell the native plants of particular regions; usually they can obtain permits for limited collecting of nonendangered species. Nursery-grown plants have a much greater rate of success than plants you collect yourself, but you will still have to make an effort to make them happy in your garden. Make sure you can provide the right living conditions for fussy specimens before you get them home.

If you know of a wildflower habitat that is in danger from development, don't simply throw yourself in front of the bulldozer. Local native plant societies or conservation groups will have better ideas about how to proceed. If there are rare or endangered species involved, they may be able to stop the development completely. Otherwise they may obtain permission to rescue plants before they are destroyed. There are now native plant societies in many states, as well as some groups that include larger regions of the country. Joining a group is one of the best ways to learn how to grow the natives of your area; meeting other enthusiasts who grow rare plants is the best way to obtain them, through seed exchanges, plants sales, and old-fashioned neighborly trade. These groups often sponsor tours so that enthusiasts can see their favorites in the wild. Admire them there, and leave them for others to enjoy.

Many horticulture societies and garden clubs are now more emphatic than they once were about the importance of preservation of native plants, but there are still members who practice exploitative collecting in the wild. Don't hesitate to speak out against such collectors, and encourage your group to censure these members. Is it worth losing friends over an ill-gotten calochortus? That is a difficult and personal decision, but you might ask yourself if your children will grow up to discover lady's slippers in the woods around you.

Today's Flowers, Tomorrow's Weeds?

FOR CENTURIES PLANTS have moved from the wild into the garden. The traffic is not entirely one way, however. We may think that we are doing nature a favor by sharing our plants with the larger landscape, but that is how weeds are born. Although many major plant invaders have been brought to us by commercial agriculture, amateur gardeners have done their part, too, to confuse the flora of our country. The pernicious polygonum, the wide-ranging water hyacinth, the rampaging purple loosestrife—all these monsters were originally offered in the guise of ornamental plants. In truth, they *are* ornamental—who has not sighed at the sight of vast waves of purple lythrum lighting up the landscape in July? If these plants had not been ornamental, attractive to buyers, easy to grow, eager to spread, we never would have had a problem with them. Problems arise when they begin to displace less aggressive natives that cannot compete for a limited habitat. We can see the same situation in the animal kingdom, where some of these conflicts are more highly publicized than the slower, more subtle confrontations of the plant world. English sparrows displace bluebirds; guppies engulf the White River spring fish in Nevada; starlings supplant just about anything.

There should be no difficult moral decisions involved in trying to limit the number of major weeds in our lives—enlightened self-interest should give us reason enough. Still, there are simple precautions we should follow, both to keep our garden flowers in line and to limit whenever we can the chances of letting loose another kudzu on the world.

There is weediness and there are weeds. A plant can be described as weedy, but that doesn't necessarily mean it wants to conquer the world.

Perennials like *Lysimachia clethroides* or *Macleaya cordata,* the plume poppy, may run rampant in your borders, but they run out of steam when they have to compete on uncultivated ground. Plants like these can be naturalized safely, although you should keep an eye on them just in case. Plants like the orange day lily and the European bellflower are in a different league; they will thrive in virtually any situation and can be removed only with the help of strong poisons. These two are, as you can see, already well established among the pantheon of major American weeds, but that doesn't keep many beginners from giving them a hand in their conquest of this continent. You help them to spread first when you invite them into your yard, and second when you belatedly try to get them out. You should not feel that because they already are a pest they are not your concern. Anything that makes it possible for a dangerous weed to move into new territory will cause problems for our native plants and for gardeners in generations to come. Anyone who has moved into a property where aegopodium has been used as a ground cover will heartily agree.

Use extreme caution with seed mixes of meadow wildflowers. Many of the species are European annuals that won't survive for long in the wild, but you could find a few hardy nuisances like oxeye daisy or lythrum. Both are rampant in the landscape already, but if you don't already have them you will deeply regret bringing them into your life.

Obey the U.S. Department of Agriculture regulations about traveling with seeds or plants. Many plant collectors consider it a great game to elude customs officials with their illegal plants. Frequently it is the same plant collectors who have despoiled wild plant populations who think nothing of smuggling their ill-gotten gains from one country to the next. These are people who feel that their private pleasures are more important than the future of the environment as a whole or the conditions of the larger world of gardening. Perhaps the chances are slim that you are bringing in deadly soil bacteria or exotic insects, but these things have happened in the past. We must share a sense of responsibility for what happens in the world of plants and show respect for any effort to protect that world. There is no problem in bringing seed from one country to another, as long as it is labeled and a list of genera is given to a USDA official for inspection. This inspection is intended to stop seed collection from endangered plants and to screen out potential weeds, and both these goals should be supported by gardeners.

. . . .

In the early centuries of gardening, the world outside the garden walls was a savage and terrifying place. One small area of cultivation represented peace and safety and order as well as food, medicine, and other essentials for life; it was an acre that man could control and make productive for his own uses. As more and more of the world has been subjected first to cultivation and then urbanization, people have come to believe that nature is at their disposal, that resources exist to be exploited, and that anything standing in the way of comfort or progress can be eliminated. It is no longer necessary for the garden to represent the triumphs of humanity. We can leave that job to massive oil refineries, to endless highways, to atomic submarines and Cruise missiles. We need our gardens now to remind us of the triumphs of nature, of the exquisite beauty of butterflies and blossoms, of the richness and complexity of the many layers of life around us—to remind us of the landscapes we may have lost forever. As California garden designer Isabelle Greene has said: "The capturing quality of a landscape, of a garden, is that it is a piece of nature that you work with, that explains nature to oneself and explains one's place in nature, explains one's situation as part of the spectrum that nature is." The garden is our opportunity to experience a world outside ourselves—a world we may have injured in the past, but which still offers mystery and delight to those who learn from it and work in it with care.

8

The Good,

or Not So Good,

Earth

. . . .

Most OF US start our gardens with remarkably little under-standing of the material that underlies it all. Soil seems the most basic "given" of a garden, the more or less brown matter beneath our property lines: what you find when you dig a hole in the ground. Digging that hole is often viewed as a rather tedious first step that must be taken, preferably by someone else, before we can get to the fun parts of gardening—choosing the plants, arranging color schemes, watching things grow. For a few years, at least, this cavalier disregard for dirt seems not to matter. Plants grow and flower, and our new borders may even seem to outshine plantings of longer history. As the plants gradually get smaller, produce fewer blooms, and appear spindly and chlorotic, the easiest solution seems to be a repetition of our earlier successful formula: let's just dig a new bed, a bigger bed, which at once grabs the spotlight while the original plantings subside into small weedy patches fading into the landscape.

We now see how ontogeny recapitulates phylogeny. Most primitive agricultural groups practiced forms of migratory farming—when the land in one area was exhausted, the tribe moved on to new territory. In more recent history, the colonization of America followed a similar pattern. Although much of the new continent was difficult to cultivate, most property was productive for at least a few years. As yields became lower, it was easier to move to a new piece of land than to labor over the old. But even the vast continent of America doesn't go on forever, and your backyard does not stretch from sea to shining sea. You have made some commitment to this property, at least to the extent of a thirty-year mortgage, and sooner or later you must focus on one spot and get serious about your soil.

Back in the days of colonization, soil science existed as little more than a few tried and true dictums handed down from one weary farmer to the next. It has only been in the last century that we have had the necessary knowledge of chemistry, the scientific apparatus, the resources, and the increasingly urgent need to discover just how complex is the ground we tred. There is no question that soil science has resulted in enormous changes in agriculture during the last hundred years, and these advances in knowledge have trickled down to amateurs as well. Today even the backyard gardener can benefit from an understanding of the proportion of hydrogen ions to hydroxyl ions. We can learn that ionic substitution of $Al+++$ for $Si+++$, and $Mg++$ or $Fe++$ for $Al+++$ is common in minerals of the 2:1 type, and discover that what we previously thought of as dirt is really Gray-Brown Podzolic soil with a distinct A_2 horizon and a B horizon that is an accumulation of sesquioxides and humus. On the other hand, when faced with such an embarrassment of information, we may be tempted to keep on digging new beds every year.

The kind of soil you have and how it behaves are the result of several factors, including: the rock from which the soil originally developed, the climate in which it was developed, the amount of organic matter that has accumulated in and on it, the kind of vegetation that has been growing on it, the slope of the land, and the drainage. And those are just some of the *natural* factors. Also to be considered are the intrusions of man: Has the soil been disturbed by house or road construction? Has it served as a dump for possibly toxic materials? Some natural and artificial conditions may have been discovered in your first years of gardening—perhaps the first time a swing of your pick unearthed a long-buried truck chassis. But there are others that don't begin to arise until your plants have been in place for a decade.

Climate and soil combine to determine the natural distribution of plants and account for many of the adaptations plants have developed in order to survive. Climate and soil have dictated the settlement of man throughout the world and the methods of cultivation developed to produce food in a variety of circumstances. Twentieth-century culture has isolated most of us from the immediate circumstances of both climate and soil so that we hardly understand how these vital factors have shaped our past and will continue to shape our future. Gardening is one of the few pursuits that can bring us back into contact with these elements; it gives us at least the chance to understand how they operate. It is only when we try to establish permanent plantings that we begin to experience the long-term effects of both climate and soil, and it is only after we have struggled with these factors for many years that we begin to understand how they affect everything we do in the garden. You probably read all about them years ago, when you couldn't have understood how crucial they are. That is why we are going to go over the basics again now, when they can make a real difference in your garden.

All that said, I have to admit to a decided preference for the specifics of climate over those of soil. I can wax enthusiastic over such details as frost dates and photoperiodicity, but soil, sadly, leaves me cold. It is hard to understand why; certainly there is more poetry to be found in Barnes loam and Sassafras sand, in Windthorst and Nimrod, in Muskingum and Kewaunee than in the blunt numerals of the climate zone system. There is the incredible detail to be discovered: The Isabella soils are generally somewhat looser and lighter in texture, with more gravel and stones than Miami loam; Brookston silty clay loam is associated with the Miami and Crosby soils, occupying the shallow sags and swales characteristic of the glacial till plain. You can learn this sort of information about your specific soil with the aid of soil maps and laboratory analysis, and it can help you to understand the vegetation patterns that flourish or fail around you. I suppose the real reason I am not enamored of soil is that understanding it only goes so far. Soil is the opposite of abstract; sooner or later you have to come down to earth, and that means work.

If many of your early plantings were trees, you might not have noticed specific problems in their growth that could be the result of soil conditions. For several reasons, trees are better suited than smaller plants to survive on poor or difficult soils. Their slow rate of growth does not make the demands upon the soil that annuals or herbaceous plants do; their strong root systems are adapted to penetrating rocky subsoil layers that would be impervious to smaller plants; their own leaves and needles supply an ever-growing layer of humus and mulch, which while nourishing its source also discourages nearby competition, as does the spreading canopy. This is why we see wonderful old trees flourishing in public parks or in cemeteries, where they have

Factors affecting soil development: prehistoric conditions; climate and drainage; geology and soil movement; previous use.

survived for generations with little or no care. This is why flowering trees and shrubs are the staples of the low-maintenance landscape and why they are so invaluable for making the framework of any garden.

Trees, and many shrubs, when properly planted in the first place, don't suffer from the kind of soil depletion created by either vegetable or perennial gardening. If you dig a big enough hole, check drainage, add organic material to the soil (even that is eschewed by some experts these days), plant the tree at the same soil level it experienced in the nursery, then water carefully for the first few months, you are off to a good start. Container propagation in this instance makes life easier for gardeners, since it provides a convenient package for planting; the tree or shrub will experience little or no root shock. A tree with sufficient sunlight and water will usually be able to make all the food it needs to grow once it is established. You can feed your trees, and if you are producing an orchard crop this might be a good idea. Fertilizing can sometimes improve the performance of flowering trees that have fallen into a pattern of flowering every two years. Also, trees under environmental stress may benefit from cautious fertilizing. But most trees and many shrubs do fine without supplements, and in difficult climates with short growing seasons, it is safer not to feed than to feed at the wrong time and risk damage to new growth late in the year.

This is not to say that trees are foolproof—you have probably killed enough of them by now to know that is not the case. But overall, it is far more likely that your fatalities among the larger woody plants were caused by lack of hardiness, disease, or physical damage than by some insufficiency of your soil. There are some trees and many shrubs that have a decided preference for soils of a specific pH (about which more anon). You may have miscalculated the drainage—this is a soil-related problem, since impermeable soil or rock layers can trap water around the roots and most trees growing in persistently damp conditions will die fairly promptly. You may not have dug deeply enough to discover an impenetrable layer of rock just below your plant's roots. A remarkable number of trees will still survive in this situation and many eventually even change it with their delving roots although they may not grow as large or as quickly as they would under better conditions.

Trees can utilize land unsuitable for general agricultural purposes, which is why, when forests are cleared for farming, the results are often disastrous. The terrible land conditions in the tropics resulting from the clearing of rain forest areas are an unhappy example. A rain forest demonstrates how a complex plant community can make the best use of a specific climate and soil situation. The dense vegetation produces enough nutritional material as it decays to sustain itself, but with the high temperatures and constant rainfall typical of the climate, the small amount of excess organic matter breaks down immediately and nutrients are quickly leached from the thin soil. When the forests are cleared, the soils are worthless. This doesn't happen only in the tropics. A dense growth of forest does not necessarily indicate deep, rich soil, as the settlers of the eastern coast of North America quickly discovered. The thin layers of forest humus that so effortlessly sustained gigantic trees are rapidly exhausted by fast-growing agricultural crops, which return nothing to the soil. And when clear-cutting occurs on a slope—the forest lands of the Northeast and the mountainous areas of the West certainly provide plenty of slopes—erosion is almost inevitable.

You may not have been slashing and burning to create your garden, but it is possible that you have been ignoring the needs of your soil. Those needs may now be making themselves felt. In a classic perennial border you are attempting to grow a large number of diverse flowering plants in a small area. This makes a huge demand upon the fertility of the soil and upon the soil's moisture content. In this way, a flowering border behaves like an agricultural crop, which drains the soil of water and nutrients in order to produce food. And as all those early settlers discovered, after a few years of producing, the soil has nothing more to give.

If you began gardening with vegetables or annuals, you may have been accustomed to turning the top six or eight inches of soil every year before you set out the plants, and you might have sprinkled around some fertilizer. But this experience gives you little help in figuring out the preparation of soil for a perennial bed, and it doesn't prepare you for the ongoing problems of soil management once the plants are in the ground.

There are several mistakes we might have made when digging the beds in the first place. Although some perennials will end up with root masses as large as those of shrubs, we tend to think of flowers as small and dig accordingly. Few first-time gardeners go deeper than eighteen inches, especially if they are accustomed to annuals or vegetables. Some go no farther than a foot, although all serious books on perennials urge three feet at least. How could a plant growing in a one-quart pot possibly need three feet of soil?

We are told to add lots of organic material. But what *is* organic material? All too often the answer is peat moss, which is about the only organic material that is commercially packaged and widely sold. Peat moss feels lovely for a while, and it may marginally improve your soil's texture if you use enough of it, but it adds virtually nothing to its fertility. If you happen to have a compost pile in operation, you have great organic material at your disposal, but the Catch-22 is that until you start to garden you don't produce any compost, so how do you start to garden? Animal manures were the time-honored solution of all those farmers in the dark ages who didn't know a hydroxyl ion from a bedbug, and they work extremely well if you are lucky enough to have a cow for a neighbor—which, sadly, is less and less likely all the time. The denatured manures sold in plastic bags have very little value as either organic matter or fertilizer.

The Best Dressed

WHETHER YOU DID it right or wrong the first time, digging the bed is only the beginning of soil management. Even a deep, well-prepared border will show signs of diminishing fertility after a few years. Oh, those lucky farmers who can plow under their acres of green cover crops; happy are the vegetable growers who blithely rototill everything for a clean slate each spring. What is one to do as the bed becomes more and more crowded with big plants ever more in need of food? We now come to the delicate question of top dressing (or side dressing, which may or may not be the same thing). Many books refer airily to this technique of soil improvement, but the term remains a password to a society of select gardeners who know what it is and how to do it but won't let on. Is it possible that sprinkling small amounts of compost among your plants is going to do any good? I used to tiptoe furtively through the beds, pressing lumps of manure into the ground wherever the space allowed. After a while I got bolder and simply threw shovelfuls at the plants late in the fall, accomplishing both top and side dressing in one blow. This seems to work quite well, although it hardly deserves such a decorous name as "dressing" ("messing" would be closer to the truth), and you might want to do it only after you are sure no one is going to visit for the rest of the year.

Inorganic fertilizers can take much of the mess out of dressing, and much of the anxiety out of plant nutrition. There is a bewildering assortment available, as a quick trip to any garden center can show you. Many provide the three essentials for plant growth, nitrogen, phosphorus, and potassium, and some supply a variety of additional trace elements as well, such as iron, sulfur, copper, or manganese. You have your choice of powder, liquid, or granules, and can select rapid- or slow-release formulas. It is unlikely that in your years of gardening you have not made use of inorganic fertilizers, but you may not understand what they can and cannot do. Complete synthetic plant foods may not be able to correct all the nutrient deficiencies to be found across America, and they may not supply everything needed by some particularly fussy plants, but they are a great boon to those of us who can never remember what elements make nitrogen unavailable, or who can't recognize a shortage of magnesium. These fertilizers contain nutrients in a soluble form that can be used by plants immediately. There are also time-release formulas that will make nutrients available slowly over the length of a growing season. Regular use of a balanced fertilizer can satisfy the nutritional needs of a wide range of plants and provide nutrients in a form that is somewhat easier to deal with than a wheelbarrow full of manure. Add some to the soil when you are preparing a bed; mix it in the soil whenever you are planting something new. If you dig it into the ground around plants in a bed, you may actually be top dressing (or is it side dressing?). It is no wonder that farmers switched wholeheartedly to synthetic fertilizers in the last decades, and it is no wonder that most gardeners believe that with a few bags of 5-10-5 around, they need never think about the soil again.

Not surprisingly, there are drawbacks to the use of synthetic fertilizers. If they are not used carefully, they can damage plants. The granular varieties should always be added to the soil in a way that prevents direct contact with roots or foliage. Foliar sprays are designed to be used on foliage, but unless they are mixed with care they can damage the leaves. It is easy to get carried away with enthusiasm and use too much fertilizer at once, which can injure or kill some plants, especially young ones. There are also strong environmental arguments against the use of chemicals to supply nutrients that can be provided by the natural processes of decay. Phosphates, in particular, can travel with runoff into the water supply and cause severe imbalances among wetland plants, fostering the growth of invasive species. In more and more agricultural areas where farmers have been dependent on synthetic fertilizers for years, devastating side effects are appearing from overuse of these products.

Inorganic fertilizers do nothing about the condition, or texture, of the soil, and soil condition is more likely to be a problem in more gardens than, say, potassium starvation. In our naive early gardening days, many of us thought that soil texture and fertility were the same thing. What we may have found, if we were using chemical fertilizers, was that we were using more and more chemicals with less results. Although fertility and texture are interrelated, they are separate characteristics and can be handled in different ways. Proper soil condition results in the right amount of air between soil particles. It ensures the best movement of water through the ground so that moisture is retained but the soil is also perfectly drained. Well conditioned soil never congeals into sullen lumps, even when stepped on, nor does it run through the fingers like beach sand. It doesn't turn into concrete when dry nor does it break into canyonlike fissures. We have all heard references to "good garden soil" on seed packets and in countless garden texts. But even after ten years of work, we may believe that our chances of finding such soil in our gardens are slightly more remote than finding a deposit of gold.

Good garden soil is made, not found. In fact, if you started with moderately good soil, it is probably less good now than when you began if you haven't been working at it. America has some of the richest and most productive soils on the planet. It also has a wild array of some of the worst soils imaginable. Your soil is probably somewhere in between, although there is more chance that it is at the difficult end of the spectrum. Almost all soils can be improved and made productive—it is merely a matter of backbreaking and time-consuming work.

The Particular Question

THE QUESTION OF sand or clay receives serious consideration by most beginners, and after several years of digging, you ought to have some idea of what you've got. Don't get distracted by the fine distinctions between sandy loam and loamy sand, between clay loam and silty clay, all precise class designations for the soil scientist. Judge instead by how your soil has behaved. If moisture seems to vanish from your garden in spite of ample watering, if unlimited amounts of compost seem to dissipate as fast as you spread them, if chemical fertilizer seems to result in wild swings between anorexia and binge eating in your plants, sandy soil is probably the reason. In many parts of the United States, thin, sandy soil combines with high rainfall to create conditions where nutrition is a constant problem. Organic matter must be added all the time, and even that doesn't seem to be often enough. In warm, humid climates, organic matter breaks down very quickly. The luxuriant growth of plants in such climates produces masses of compost, but the rate of decay is equally high, so new material must be added frequently. One advantage of sandy soil is that it takes less fertilizer to feed your plants, but the down side is that even a small excess is more dangerous. Also, although a little fertilizer goes a long way in sand, a little rain can wash the nutrients down the drain before your plants get their first meal. The use of mulches is particularly important in the soils and climates of this type because a strong material such as pine needles, oak leaves, or wood chips will slow the movement of rainfall, resist evaporation, and cool the soil—all of which will slow the leaching of nutrients and the breakdown of organic matter. These surface mulches will themselves eventually break down and become a beneficial part of the soil.

Conditioning sandy soil sounds like a lot of work. But those of us who struggle with clay think we have a much harder time of it. Although the differences between sand and clay are usually described in terms of the size of the soil particles, this doesn't really give any sense of how the different soils behave. A particle of sand is completely different from a particle of clay, not just in size or weight but in its molecular structure and its ability to react with water, minerals, and other particles of clay. You may think that a lump of clay is the ultimate inert object, but in the world of soils, clay is known for its abundant activity. Although the chemistry is fascinating, you don't have to understand ion exchange to know how clay works. It sticks. It sticks to itself, it sticks to water, it sticks to shovels and shoes and paws and rocks, and it is a pretty poor gardener who hasn't figured that out in a few years of digging. Clearly these two soil types could not appear more different, so it is hard to understand that the solution to soil improvement is the same for both. Compost, animal manure, organic material, humus— call it what you will, it is what all soils need.

Let us take a moment to clarify our terms. English books tend to refer to all organic soil additives as manures. In America, manures refer to animal wastes used for soil improvement; compost is the term applied to any other organic material which is processed through decay to make humus.

When I was a child in the early fifties, we were not the only family in our neighborhood to have a garden. We were, however, the only family with a compost pile. This was so much a part of our lives that it was many years before I realized that "compost pile" was not an everyday household term like "driveway" or "front door." It was rather a delicious place for children and not at all dirty, at least by a child's reckoning. We marveled at the heat produced by disintegrating grass clippings, and delighted in the endless supply of worms. I was quite unaware of the care with which my father managed it and rather took for granted that any pile of leaves and weeds could produce a seemingly endless supply of rich, dark dirt.

The compost piles of contemporary organic gardening sound much more intimidating, with constant demands for turning and aeration, with the possibilities of either too much water or too little, too high a temperature or too low, too much nitrogen or not enough. It is really simpler than that. If you pile up your leaves, grass clippings, weeds, dead flowers, and kitchen wastes, they will gradually decay and produce compost, usually in less than a year. Chopping the material will make it decay faster, as will keeping it constantly moist. A sustained temperature of 140°F will speed disintegration and supposedly incapacitate weed seeds, but don't count on it—even if you *could* ascertain the temperature of your pile (with a meat thermometer, perhaps?) and keep it constant, you should not assume that all remnants of weeds have been destroyed, either roots or seeds, so take care to separate out the most invasive species. Even tiny root fragments of aegopodium, creeping bellflower, Japanese knotweed, and other invasive plants can survive and carry the plague to other parts of the garden, so take care. Tough, dry, woody stems take a long time to break down; shred them, burn them, or confine them to another pile.

Since most residential communities have banned leaf burning, many local governments have established composting programs on a grand scale. The resulting humus is then available to residents. If your town has such a program, grab your wheelbarrow and head on down to collect. Even better is the fact that some towns provide compost seminars to school groups and interested individuals who were deprived of the compost experience in their childhoods.

Even if you have been disorganized about managing your garden waste for the last decade, you still may have something to show for it. Dig down under the piles of debris—you may be astonished to find that composting has been going on without you. This long-decayed humus won't have the kind of nutrients that more recently decomposed matter can provide, but it is still excellent for soil condition. If produced and used properly, compost alone can provide most of the nutrients needed by plants, and that is the aim of the organic-gardening enthusiasts. It is partially decayed compost that is most beneficial, since the nutrients are released by the process of decay. But if you don't want to worry about whether you have enough nitrogen or phosphorus, sparing applications of inorganic fertilizer will take care of that anxiety, leaving you to enjoy your compost for all the other good it can do.

Home composting can be an important way to reduce the amount of garbage we must dispose of in landfills, which is why many town sanitation operations are interested in promoting it. It is astonishing to see how much kitchen refuse can be used in this beneficial way once you have a system established. In our family, a combination of composting and recycling reduced our garbage to less than a quarter of what it had been. You can make compost in garbage cans or large plastic bags in even the smallest urban backyard. Through catalogs there are a variety of premade composters available that make the whole process almost decorative. For several reasons it may be best not to include meat trimmings or bones in your pile; they are very slow to disintegrate and are attractive to scavengers, which may even include your own pet. Even without meat, your compost can become the haunt of raccoons and skunks; I am very cautious about adding to the pile after dark.

I must admit that, although I make a great deal of compost, I mostly use manure. In part, I use it because I have a barn full of it; in part, because my own composting is rather haphazard; in part because I just like it. For years I followed the old adage that said that while cow manure could be used immediately, horse manure had to be aged. I have gotten less and less cautious about this, and although I still don't dig it in absolutely fresh it certainly is usable after a month or so. To further my research in the matter, the horses periodically wander through the garden and distribute some very fresh samples, not one of which, as far as I can tell, has ever killed a plant. (The usual caution against horse manure is actually directed against the use of stable bedding with a high content of straw, which should be allowed to break down before being used.) Experiment with more obscure manures with caution. Fresh poultry droppings, for instance, can be toxic to plants and can do some harm to human beings who shovel them around.

Once you have your compost or manure, use it liberally. Organic material, unlike synthetic fertilizers, can be used in unlimited amounts without danger of burning. Regardless of your soil type, compost will bring it closer to that ever-elusive goal, good garden soil. It will improve the drainage of heavy soils while retaining water in sand. It will make acid soil less acid and alkaline soil less salty. Organic material can hardly be described as a quick fix, since nothing about soil is quick, but it can make a greater improvement in your garden than any other single element. All you have to do is make it, or get it, and use it.

Using it, though, has its own problems. We have already discussed top dressing, which is particularly worthwhile on light, sandy soils. And it goes without saying that compost should be added every time a new plant is planted, every time an old plant is divided. But even that is not enough. Every so often, the entire bed should be redone, as we mentioned when we discussed the perennial border. This advice comes as a blow to those who thought that a perennial bed meant the same thing as a permanent bed. Every seven to ten years you must be prepared to haul all the plants out, dig up the entire space, bring in masses of compost, and start over. If you have not done this once already, here is your chance to dig your bed the way it should have been done the first time—all the way down to three feet. A complete overhaul on a regular schedule will work wonders for your soil condition. Most beds should get it at least every ten years. (Obviously some big feeders like clematis or roses can't be lifted, and must depend on top dressing, supplemented with liquid or granular fertilizer.)

As I said, my composting is haphazard at best, but it does eventually produce humus. Last year, when I was transplanting some conifers, I needed additional dirt to fill in around them and used my compost. This year the bare patch of soil surrounding the evergreens exploded with bloom. It was like a reunion of all the plants I had ever discarded, weeds and choice ornamentals combined. There were bright yellow candelabra verbascums flowering at eye level, brilliant blue echium, purple hesperis, Queen Anne's lace, and a regal silver thistle eight feet high. No Meadow-in-a-Can ever produced such an eccentric selection. (The conifers, needless to say, were invisible.) The effect was completely unintentional and immensely comical to me, since it was abundant, blooming proof of how disorganized my gardening is. (I suppose I ought to be embarrassed.) Most visitors seem to think that it is just another new bed in progress, which I suppose it is. The point of this confession is to show that composting does not destroy seeds and compost sure does make things grow.

One mystery may puzzle you as you dig up the old beds: where did all the rocks come from? I used to think, as I dug out beds I had made in my gardening adolescence, that I must have been an idiot to leave in so many big rocks. How could I have overlooked these chunks, which range in size from tennis ball to basketball? Now that some of these beds are getting their third or fourth face-lift, I no longer wonder. I may be an idiot for gardening here in the first place, but there was a time when these beds were free of rocks. Not for long, however. Rocks are thrust up through the lower layers of subsoil by frost heaving, and an open, porous, beautifully conditioned layer of flower bed seems to make it even easier for boulders to become upwardly mobile.

Although compost and other organic soil additives will not burn plants as inorganic fertilizers sometimes do, this does not necessarily mean that high fertility is desirable for all types of plants. Many classic border perennials are "big feeders" and will thrive on a rich diet, but numerous native plants, woodland species, and alpines require quite the opposite. Many trees and shrubs appear to be less hardy if they are too well fed, and many plants suffer severe damage if they are fed too late in the growing season. Often overfed plants are weak-stemmed, with a tendency to topple; sometimes a plant will produce luxuriant leaves and few flowers—classic symptoms of too much nitrogen. Remember that very well rotted compost and aged manure will improve soil texture without adding to fertility if it looks as if some specimens ought to be on a diet.

Often it is too much to ask that all the plants you want to grow be happy in one big border with uniform fertility. As you gradually renovate the beds of your youth, create some with leaner soil to accommodate species with more spartan tastes. Native woodland plants will grow best in soil as close as possible to that of a native woodland. And you may want to establish some areas for plants that love or loathe lime.

The Acid Test

WE HAVE ARRIVED at the topic of pH, which I have handily avoided until now. Perhaps after your years of gardening you know roughly if your soil is acid or alkaline. Or you may have no idea. I know successful gardeners who are in the last category, and less successful ones who know their pH reading to the second decimal place. The pH scale, as I'm sure you are already aware, is the measure of hydrogen ion activity in the soil. The scale runs from 1 to 14, with acid soils measuring from 1 to 6, alkaline soils from 14 to 8, and a neutral midpoint of 7. Soil's pH affects the availability of nutrients and also influences the action of bacteria at work on organic material. For both these important functions the ideal pH is between 5.8 and 7—that is, between slightly acid to neutral. This is also the range that will satisfy the greatest number of plants. With soil in that range, you don't have anything to worry about, if all you want to do is grow a great number of beautiful flowers.

For a surprising number of gardeners, however, that isn't enough. There are certain plants they want to grow that are not happy with a blandly neutral soil—plants that demand exotic extremes of acidity or those that languish without lime. And there are also great numbers of gardeners whose soil does not fall into that happy medium, gardeners who don't want to be limited to the few species that will tolerate white alkali that is a perfect 10, or the pine-barren soils at around 3.

Most gardeners at one time or another go through a stage of being convinced that all their failures are due to some esoteric mineral imbalance in their soil. The obvious answer to this kind of paranoia is to have a soil test. Not just the do-it-yourself type where you press litmus papers into the ground and then argue with your partner for twenty minutes over whether the color that comes up is pink or blue. What you need is a real laboratory analysis that will settle, once and for all, just how much molybdenum you've got and respond to your suspicions about boron. The results may be as fascinating as the discovery of your level of high-density lipoproteins and will probably change your gardening just as much. Unless you live in a pine barren or a salt flat, you will probably find that your soil falls within a reasonable range. A reasonable range may not be the perfect medium we mentioned earlier, but even soils between 7 and 8.5 will support a wide range of plants, as will those between 5 and 6.5. Only acidity below 4 and alkalinity above 9 are directly toxic to most plants, but the pH has many indirect effects on soil nutrients. Increasing acidity makes calcium and magnesium less available; high alkalinity makes iron, manganese, copper, zinc, and possibly boron harder for plants to utilize.

If you do live in a pine barren or a salt flat, or if you simply want to change the soil you have to accommodate plants you can't grow, you can add limestone to acid soil and use sulfur on alkali. There are also special fertilizers constructed with chelated minerals that make iron, zinc, and manganese available for plants even in the highly alkaline soils of the West. Once again, all these additives will work best when added with organic soil conditioners. Keep in mind that changing the pH even a small amount requires a lot of whichever additive you are using. It is also not a one-time job, but a constant struggle against the persistent chemistry of the surrounding soil and the water you use. You will need to keep testing your soil and adjusting the pH accordingly. If you are trying to grow just a few plants with a recognizable preference, your efforts may be best expended by creating a raised bed with a specific soil mix that can be adjusted in any way you like, and that will keep any extra hydroxyl ions from coming or going.

Impermeable clay soils with high alkalinity are frequently found in the semiarid areas of the western United States and present the most common form of an extreme pH problem. But even with intractable caliche, the basic process of soil improvement is the same: constant additions of organic material will open the soil, promote drainage, and slowly neutralize alkaline elements; improved drainage and careful irrigation will leach excess salts from the ground and prevent buildup; chelated fertilizers will make iron and other minerals available to plants. Books from the excellent Sunset series go into more specifics than I will here. Although soil work will gradually improve the condition of the ground and alleviate the extremes of alkalinity, you will still have a long way to go before you can expect azaleas to flourish in these conditions. Bizarrely enough, there seem to be unlimited numbers of gardeners who want to grow nothing else. The best way to deal with any extreme soil condition, or even not such extreme soil conditions, is to find plants that will thrive in the soil you have, rather than to aspire to plants and soil you will never achieve.

The pH factor often becomes of greater interest to gardeners when they want to go beyond the most familiar and accommodating plants. But it is worth keeping in mind that more challenging plants may be fussy about many aspects of their growing conditions, not just pH. A gardener in Nevada can laboriously acidify a bed for ericaceous plants, but she may not be able to provide the cool, humid climate some of those plants require. One friend of mine who had killed several lovely clethra was inclined to blame it on his limestone soil. When closely questioned he admitted that a dry, gravelly location might have been equally at fault. As any of us who struggle to grow the beautiful flowers of the Rockies can attest, creating the proper alkaline soil is only the first step, and often the only one we can control. How are we to prevent the hot, muggy weather that frequently spells the end to our efforts at *Eritrichium nanum*? Was it the wrong pH that did in my oxytropis, or did I neglect to add the selenium some of these species require? Some gardeners, and many gardening books, like to emphasize pH because it is something we can know and alter and manipulate to our own ends. But a perfect pH will not guarantee you the raoulia of your dreams, and the wrong pH should not be a scapegoat for all your failures.

Better soil will not guarantee that we can grow everything we desire, but it will expand the range of planting possibilities far beyond what we can manage in our gardens. There is a great deal more that we can learn about our soils, and you might now be inspired to dig more deeply into the science of dirt. I have barely touched upon the behavior of leguminous cover crops, and perhaps you will have more success than I at understanding cation-exchange capacity. The sight of a sentence containing $\frac{[H+]}{\sqrt{[Ca++]}}$ = constant is enough to send me out to the manure pile in a hurry. I really must get on with my top dressing.

9

A Hard,

Cold Look at

Hardiness

....

．．

It IS PART of your standard induction package into the world of gardening, that map of America transversed with swathes of dots and dashes that become particularly obscure as they converge on the location of your property. Perhaps you found it in your first seed catalog; certainly it occupied half a page in your first gardening book (unless you started, as I did, with the loquacious Beverly Nichols). It is your official United States Department of Agriculture Plant Hardiness Zone Map. Did you sweep by it in impatience in those early days, or did you seize it with the excitement with which one first discovers the astrological calendar? Just as a star sign was going to reveal the inner truths of your personality, so the magic zone number would uncover the mysteries of our American climate and make gardening safe and easy forever.

It goes without saying that the hardiness map is an American invention. If you were nurtured with English gardening books, you may have thought a hardy plant was one that would take a little frost, like maybe rosemary or agapanthus. This is fine if you live in California, but you suffered a rude awakening if you applied the English views of hardiness to gardening in Chicago. It was in order to avoid this kind of disaster that Alfred Rehder in 1927 created a hardiness map for his *Manual of Cultivated Trees and Shrubs*. But it was Donald Wyman who made the hardiness map and its accompanying Zone System an important part of American gardening. In *Hedges, Screens and Windbreaks* (1938), Wyman took data from the U.S. weather bureau records from 1895 to 1935 and constructed a map based on the average annual minimum temperatures. Because he was at the Arnold Arboretum for much of his productive life, and because his many books were published there, this map was known as the Arnold Arboretum hardiness map. Wyman's books reached—and continue to reach—a very wide audience, in popular gardening as well as in commercial horticulture. They were extremely influential in spreading the idea of the zone system.

In 1960, the Department of Agriculture published its own map and zone system. It was based on the same data Wyman used, but eliminated some of the idiosyncrasies of the earlier system by creating zones with a uniform range of ten degrees. For years the two maps existed side by side (Wyman made his last update in 1971) and may have caused as much confusion as they eliminated during that period. They looked nearly identical, but assigned different zones to different areas. But now the Arnold map is gone, and in 1990 the USDA published its latest update, a four-by-four-foot full-color beauty featuring Mexico and Canada as well as ever more exact details of our own states, county by county. (It is available from the Superintendent of Documents, U.S. Printing Office, Washington, D.C., for $6.50.)

You may have followed one of the available versions of a hardiness map during your first years of gardening, and you may have found that it was helpful in some cases, and useless in others. One reason for this uneven success is that no single system can account for the many aspects of climate, all of which influence the distribution of plants in different ways. Another reason may have been a limited understanding of your specific climate. Very few nongardeners have a detailed knowledge of weather; it is only by spending years outside that you begin to know how cold it can get, how hot it can be, when to expect wet weather, and when to prepare for drought. Weather is the all-important context of gardening, and most of us develop an almost morbid fascination with it once we start paying attention. How many of your neighbors can tell you if it rained in the last ten days? A gardener can tell you the precipitation total to within a tenth of an inch. The average American has only the vaguest idea of when the first frost might occur in his region—a gardener can tell you when frost first hit in each of the past seven years. You didn't have that kind of information when you started out. If you have it now, you may not know how to use it. This is why, even though hardiness seems the most basic topic covered in every beginner text, we are going to go back over it again. Like many of the most basic topics, climate is a lot more complicated than we thought back in the days when we first tried to grow bougainvillaea outdoors in Detroit. Once you have a more complete understanding of how climate works, you can use your growing body of knowledge about your own particular microclime to succeed with plants you thought would never survive—even to succeed with plants you lost the first time out. You cannot change your climate, but you can learn to modify its effects on your garden.

The hardiness map does not pretend to answer all our questions about climate, as the USDA makes quite clear: "Survival of landscape plants over winter was selected as the most critical criterion in their adaptation to the environment." Cold hardiness, then, is what this map is about, since that is the major, unchangeable climate factor we have to endure in most parts of this country. Cold is not the only weather-related reason plants fail to survive, but it certainly accounts for more fatalities than any other single factor. And survival is not even enough to satisfy the USDA. They go on to say that "the zone ratings were intended to indicate *excellent adaptability* of the plants. Many plants may survive in warmer or colder zones. Usually, mere survival does not represent satisfactory performance"—an opinion you may endorse after clearing out the half-dead "survivors" from your first years of gardening. Because of this qualification, the flowering dogwood receives a Zone 5 rating; it will survive in Zone 4 but not bloom, because the flower buds are more sensitive to severe cold than the rest of the plant. *Rosa multiflora,* wildly invasive and apparently indestructible in Zone 5, is equally indestructible in Zone 4. But it dies back to the roots in colder climates, leaving a dead mass of thorny branches, like a thicket of barbed wire, and blooms about one year in six. The USDA, like any sane gardener, does not consider this a "satisfactory performance" and rates it Zone 5.

It is a relatively simple task to study the map and find your magic number. You can then double-check by reading over the list of minimal temperatures for each zone. But discovering your zone is a little like discovering your astrological sign. It is, of course, fascinating to know you are an Aries living in Zone 7, but what then? You still have to find the career or investment or lover that is right for an Aries, and you still have to find the plants that will live in Zone 7, and that is where both systems run into trouble. A supermarket pamphlet tells you a Gemini is right for you; the local newspaper says to seek out a Sagittarius. One authoritative volume tells you you can't grow eucalyptus in Atlanta, while some enthusiastic catalog suggests you try it in Philadelphia. The zone ratings for individual plants are the result of accumulated data from many sources. Botanical gardens, arboretums, and commercial growers have been keeping statistics for years on what will survive in their particular area, but when one individual or organization attempts to analyze all the information, the results can be anything but definitive. Because of Wyman's work, we have fairly solid ratings for most of the major ornamental trees and shrubs that he describes, but although his information is very good for hardiness in the Northeast, it can be questionable in other parts of the country. Catalogs from small nurseries that grow most of their own woody plant material are usually very helpful for their locale, but some big mail-order operations can be optimistic to the point of dishonesty. And when it comes to rating herbaceous plants, the zone system is still something of a free-for-all.

For those of you not quite comfortable playing the numbers, the hardiness map offers a list of "indicator plants" that might help you understand what zone you are in. If you see boxwood and English ivy but not Atlas cedars in your neighborhood, you are probably in Zone 6; pittosporums and olearias suggest Zone 8. Paper birch and *Cornus canadensis*? Welcome to Zone 2. These observations are helpful because they encourage us to recognize the natural and artificial microclimes that exist within each zone—even when we might not know our exact temperature range—as well as to recognize when one zone modulates into the next. For example, I can find *Magnolia soulangiana,* rated Zone 5, flowering in towns twenty miles from my garden in every direction, but my own is a stunted, half-dead survivor that has bloomed once in twenty years. What factors are at work here that could make such a difference? If the protection offered by clusters of buildings in even a small town makes a big difference to some borderline species, the region is most likely on the edge between two temperature zones. Further evidence can be seen if the forsythia and flowering quince bloom only six or eight inches above the ground—that is, in only those areas that have been covered with snow all winter. From these clues and from observation of other plants, we might conclude that the garden is in Zone 4 most winters, but we might also decide that some modifications could enable certain Zone 5 plants to succeed here.

Through the use of indicator plants, we begin to realize that hardiness is not an abstract concept, the result of numbers and graphs. The climate of a particular area and the plants' abilities to adapt to the characteristics of that climate result in the living landscape we see. We should all become more alert to both the natural and artificial range of the plants around us. Even if we cannot at first identify all the plants we are seeing, we can start to recognize patterns in their distribution. Any routine drive or tedious commute can gain interest as we start to analyze the landscape speeding by. See how certain species cluster in low, damp areas, and how others are only found on the north slope of the hillsides? What does it mean when a plant you haven't seen in a hundred miles suddenly starts appearing again? When a mixed hardwood forest gives way to conifers and birches or the flowering dogwoods in the understory are replaced by shadblow, there are climate and geographical factors at work that may affect what we plant.

Cold Facts

PLANTS ARE SUSCEPTIBLE to cold in different ways. Some will tolerate frost, but not freezing of the roots. Rosemary is a good example of this sensitivity, as are many plants considered to be hardy in English gardens. Some freezing temperatures occur there, but the soil does not turn into a block of concrete for five months, as it does in much of the United States. As we mentioned earlier, some plants, such as dogwood and forsythia, have hardy stems and roots, but tender buds that may not withstand the winter. Some plants survive freezing if they are shaded, but perish if they freeze in full sun. Some can take the cold as long as there is no wind.

In freezing weather, water freezes in the spaces between the cells of the plant tissue. This freezing draws water out of the cells and creates a beneficial layer that slows transpiration and prevents rapid temperature change within the cells. The thick, reduced liquid that remains within the cells has a much lower freezing point, although it can still eventually freeze. The point at which the cellular fluid freezes varies from plant to plant, which is why some plants will tolerate temperatures of twenty below zero but perish at twenty-five below. But the absolute temperature is not the only damaging factor, nor is the freezing of cellular tissue the only way a plant can be damaged in winter. Even during dormancy, plants are transpiring and losing water. If too much water is lost from the intercellular layer, water will be lost in turn from the plant cells, and damage will occur. This is particularly likely to happen when the ground is exposed and frozen because the roots of the plant cannot take up moisture from the soil to replace lost fluids. A great deal of winter damage is the result of dehydration—those dried-out-looking plants that died last winter really *were* dried out. Bright sunlight and strong winds are additional factors that can contribute to dehydration, and they contribute to other forms of damage as well. You have probably seen long, vertical cracks in the bark of trees and shrubs that suffered during the winter. Notice how this condition is usually found on the side of the plant facing the sun. When the temperature in the cells of the bark changes too rapidly, those cells rupture. Wrapping the trunks of trees, especially those that are young or newly planted, gives some measure of protection. (There is a paperlike material sold for the purpose, or you can use burlap strips. These materials also provide some protection from bark-gnawing pests, which can girdle your trees.) On conifers, you may see brown needles on the south side, another result of the same problem. Planting susceptible material out of direct winter sun can make a big difference. Shrubs of borderline hardiness, such as rhododendrons, are much more likely to survive if they are growing in light shade. Winter sun is dangerous in two ways: it makes the outer layer of bark or leaves change temperature quickly, and it dries necessary moisture from plant surfaces. Wind also can be fatal because of desiccation, particularly to broadleaf evergreens, although a surprising number of conifers can also be injured by winter drying.

Quite a bit of borderline material can survive if protected from both sun and wind. You can create artificial windbreaks and sunscreens of burlap and plastic, but strategic planting furnishes a more permanent and decorative line of defense. Use trees and shrubs of proven hardiness to provide wind-breaks for more vulnerable species. A windbreak doesn't have to be a solid wall of evergreens—a broken line of plants of varying heights is more attractive and offers the most protection. Create an understory layer of plants that can benefit from the presence of tall, deciduous trees above them. This kind of naturalistic setting is the most attractive for many broadleaf evergreens, and it gives them a much greater chance of survival.

Mulching helps to prevent winter injury in several ways. A thick layer of mulch on the surface keeps frost out while holding water in. By slowing the evaporation of water from the soil surface, mulch ensures that water is available for roots throughout the winter. In places where snow cover is sparse and episodic, mulch is an especially important tool. It is also invaluable for preventing too-rapid warming of the soil in early spring. If you started out with a vegetable garden, you were probably interested in getting the soil warmed up for planting as early as possible in spring. With perennial herbaceous plants and bulbs, early thawing is not desirable, since it sends new growth shooting above ground where it can be snapped by an unexpected freeze. There is no advantage to getting your perennials out of the gate in record time; they will catch up quickly enough when the weather is ready for them and when they are ready for spring.

Sometimes our own solicitude for our plants can be fatal. Watering and fertilizing are fine early in the season, but if you keep it up through late summer in a climate where winter arrives early, the lush new growth prompted by all that food and water will die back with the first solid freeze. Late-season pruning can also force new growth at a time when it can be dangerous. Soft, new growth on a woody plant is much more susceptible to freezing than mature growth because it has a higher percentage of water in the cells; the shock caused by rapid growth followed by rapid dieback can kill the entire plant. In areas of early freezing, don't fertilize in August, don't water heavily, and don't plant trees and shrubs late in autumn. Sure, all the books recommend major landscape planting throughout the fall, but if your winter arrives sometime in October, most of your September-planted specimens won't live to see the spring.

The Hardiness Zone Map may tell you about the severity of your winter, but it will say nothing about its duration. There are, in fact, separate maps that detail the frost dates across America. But once again, they can offer only generalizations. Frost is notoriously local in its effects—you can see in your

own garden how one area might be completely white, while a few feet away most of the plants are untouched. It is also surprising to find that many beginning gardeners don't understand how the length of the growing season can affect plant selection. With annuals and vegetables the equation is pretty straightforward: it doesn't take long to figure out that if melons take 106 days to mature and your frost-free season is 90 days, melons are out of the question. But the effects of late and early frost on herbaceous and woody material may be so subtle that you miss the symptoms. June-flowering lilies affected by frost can look as if they have been struck by disease—the tips of the shoots turn watery and yellow or brown, become twisted and mal-formed, and don't bloom—although the bulbs will usually continue to grow and may bloom another year. The growing tips of the lilacs turn black, the new flowers wither without opening. Sometimes you don't see the damage for months, as when flowering fruit trees that have been frozen fail to produce later in the summer.

Frost at the end of the season can do more than simply shorten the span of the impatiens. Trees and shrubs planted for decorative autumn fruit and foliage can be decidedly undecorative when hit by early freezing. How often have I admired the brilliant late show of the many crab apples that enrich gardens in the milder parts of the Northeast. But my spectacular "Golden Hornet," covered with fat yellow fruit in August, was covered with fat brown mush two weeks later after temperatures ventured into the twenties. Some varieties of *Ilex verticillata* keep glowing red berries well into December; some keep little black lumps instead, if it gets too cold too soon. Since this nondescript shrub is grown only for its winter effect, it behooves one to get the cultivar that will fit the clime.

The speed with which a plant starts growing in spring can determine whether it will suffer from frost. Species that greet April with a great burst of activity are easy targets for the frosts of May, while slow starters like platycodon or *Asclepias tuberosa,* which appear so late you are always sure you have lost them, seldom get hit. For this reason, climates where nothing warms up until May are often easier on plants than areas where periods of freezing and thawing alternate through the spring. The plants are protected as long as they are dormant. This is why more plants are lost in spring than in winter, and this is another reason for winter mulching. A heavy cover of branches or leaves keeps the soil from warming and starting to thaw, and keeps plants dormant as long as possible. But there are some plants that will get off to an early start no matter what we do, and these are best abandoned by those of us with late-spring freezing. At the other end of the season, the rate at which a plant prepares for winter can be as crucial as its temperature tolerance once it is dormant. Often a species from a long-summer climate does not slow its growth rate in time to survive early freezing; this makes a bad candidate for a climate with only ninety frost-free days.

Photo Opportunities

ONE FACTOR AT work in determining when a plant starts to go dormant is photoperiodicity, which is the intimidating term that refers to the effect the length of the days has upon certain plants. You have heard of photoperiodicity if you ever tried to find out how to make last year's poinsettia turn red again. The process is incredibly tedious: you have to move it in and out of a closet each day according to a complicated schedule, which convinces the plant that the days are actually getting shorter (or longer—I can never remember, because lugging a poinsettia around can make any day seem longer). Some plants are extremely responsive to this factor; on others it seems to have little or no effect. Day length can influence any number of key events in a plant's life: when it flowers, how long it takes to set seed or fruit, when it starts to go dormant. We may have noticed that while certain plants can flower late or early depending on the temperatures that season, some plants are so rigidly on schedule that they often start flowering on the same day from year to year. The latter are the ones controlled by photoperiodicity.

The chrysanthemum can provide a familiar illustration of the frustrations of photoperiodicity combined with climate. It will flower only in the relatively short days of declining summer, which is ideal for those with a leisurely fall season ahead of them. For those of us up north, the first frost arrives long before the short days, so the chrysanthemum, which is not particularly hardy, seldom provides the glory it offers to milder regions.

Lugging one poinsettia around is bad enough; if you try to influence photoperiodicity in your garden you are really taking on an impossible project. You can tuck your chrysanthemums under a cozy quilt every night, but you should ask yourself if one plant is really worth that kind of effort. We can't change our day length out-of-doors, but we can try to understand why it may make certain plants difficult for us to grow. For instance, some plants from the southern hemisphere, even if they are cold hardy enough to live in our climate, may simply be on such a different light schedule that we cannot hope to make them comfortable. Since photoperiodicity is merely one factor influencing only some plants, we should not be discouraged from trying species from radically different parts of the world, but we must keep it in mind when other explanations for disaster fail.

Heat Waves

THE USDA HARDINESS Zone Map does not take on the question of heat tolerance in plants. Those of us who deal with subzero temperatures part of the year tend to dismiss this topic, but it is a major factor in many parts of the United States, and even in temperate areas it can affect the performance of certain plants. We may assume that any plant that will survive in chilly Zone 2 will be grateful for conditions in Zone 6, but this is anything but the case with, for example, *Cornus canadensis*. We mentioned above that this lovely native ground cover is an indicator plant for Zone 2. You may find it in some Zone 4 corners of the Adirondacks, but try to move it to the comparatively tropical regions around New York City and you are bound for failure. This is not one of those plants that simply have not been tried in different climates; a great many knowledgeable gardeners have tried it without success. Like a number of appealing far-north plants, the pretty bunchberry has very little heat tolerance. For this plant, almost anything over seventy degrees counts as heat, which means limited success in most of the climates where people prefer to live.

Heat intolerance is a factor often overlooked by those in the central United States who experience the typical extremes of a continental climate. In choosing plants from the far north that will survive Zone 4 winters, gardeners in, say, Nebraska may not realize that some natives of inland Alaska won't endure the persistent heat of a Midwest summer. There are not as many definitive clues to death from heat intolerance as there are from cold, and one misleading factor is that often the plant doesn't die in the summer. It sort of limps along, looking miserable but alive, until the winter—*then* it dies. Other symptoms of heat intolerance are leaf discoloration, stunted growth or too-rapid growth followed by dieback, and premature dropping of buds, flowers, or fruit. For some plants, even a short period of high temperatures is fatal. Others can survive such periods, but cannot endure a location where the temperature does not fall at night. Sometimes a northern native can't take the prolonged growing seasons available in the South or California; this can result in short lives for herbaceous plants and badly scrambled blooming periods for trees and shrubs. The Sunset gardening books, intended as they are for the western regions of the country, take heat seriously, so they are a good source of information on the topic. Their own highly detailed version of a hardiness map and zone system, not surprisingly, has nothing in common with the USDA system, so it must be taken as a self-contained unit. (Be warned that, in spite of the prevalence of the USDA map, there are still many books and catalogs whose authors seem to think they have come up with a more exact measure of hardiness. These idiosyncratic zone maps are a distracting nuisance since they work against the establishment of a system we can all follow.) More and more books are now including some indication of heat tolerance in their ratings of plants.

Water: Too Much and Too Little

A N Y O N E   W H O   H A S ever muttered, "It's not the heat; it's the humidity," has recognized that temperature is only one part of weather. Water is the other significant factor in climate: water in the atmosphere, water going into the atmosphere through evaporation, water coming out of the atmosphere as precipitation. We all know how vital water is for plant life, but we might not understand some of the ways water works with temperature to limit what we can grow.

Some plants are extremely sensitive to humidity in the air. Often these are the high-alpine gems beloved by rock gardeners, but there are some lowland plants that suffer as well. Plants that have evolved drought-resistant mechanisms that enable them to survive in desert climates can find these mechanisms working against them when they encounter the typically muggy climates of eastern North America. Furry foliage designed to trap and utilize every drop ends up sodden as blotting paper. Low transpiration rates, which preserve moisture in thin mountain air, can suffocate alpines brought against their wills to lower elevations and higher humidity. You can improve drainage and keep water away from the sensitive crowns, but like photoperiodicity humidity is a factor difficult to change in a whole garden. Yes, some fanatics do move their eritrichiums into air-conditioned houses for July and August, but that may not be the way most of us live. Plant selection is the only answer, determined by a lot of trial and error.

Because of the droughts suffered in different parts of America over the last decade, we tend to think of shortages as the major problem water can cause for gardeners. But principles of irrigation were mastered in the first centuries of agriculture. There may not be much water, and there are any number of reasons for not using limited water supplies for ornamental horticulture, but we do know a great deal about how to store water, how to move it, how to get it to the places we want it. We have been somewhat less successful in dealing with too much water.

A great many plants survive better in a cold dry climate than in a cold wet one. I remember how astonished I was on my first visit to the northern Rockies. The gardens of Montana and Wyoming were filled with perennials I knew were not hardy in my garden back east, where winter temperatures were not nearly so severe. Dry winter soil and ample snow cover were two factors that accounted for the success of these gardens; the opposite conditions back east spell disaster for many of us.

It may seem paradoxical that dry winter soil should be desirable, after our discussion of the perils of dehydration. But the dry western soils are not bone-dry in winter. Slowly melting snow provides the small amounts of moisture needed by roots during dormancy. The snow also keeps the soil at a constant temperature that is a great deal warmer than the air around it, and it prevents the alternating freezing and thawing that cause so much damage in more moderate regions.

One result of excess moisture in the soil in winter is frost heaving. The freezing and thawing of water in the soil make ice crystals that expand, then melt, causing the soil to thrust up, then subside, leaving cracks and mounds, and thrusting some plants completely out of the ground. Certain plants—many species of primroses, for instance—are very prone to this. Others are subject to this kind of injury only when they are young or recently planted. In early spring you can find the poor victims lying on top of the ground, their roots exposed. Occasionally, if they are tough and you are careful, you can stick them back in and cover them up, but you should expect to sustain some losses from this misfortune each spring. Such damage won't be so evident with trees and shrubs, but the roots of larger woody plants can still suffer from heaving, especially in the first years after planting.

We can't do much to limit the amount of rain that goes into the soil each year, but we can act to make sure the moisture only stays as long as it is needed. Soil condition and drainage act together to control the amount and the movement of moisture in the soil. Drainage is as simple as plumbing and as vital. Water will move down into the ground as far as it can go, but soil conditions often dictate that this is not far enough to keep it from gathering in pools around the roots of your plants. When water fills up the air spaces in the soil, the roots can no longer function, and the plant dies. The simplest principles of both drainage and plumbing are keep the water moving and make it go where you want it to go. Sometimes that requires digging down and breaking up layers of impermeable subsoil. It could mean planting on a slope or at the top of a retaining wall. In desperate circumstances it could mean laying a course of drainage tile beneath your beds.

Keep in mind when you are calculating the drainage of an area that roads, sidewalks, driveways, and other forms of construction will often keep the water from moving in the desired direction and may even direct water from their surfaces into places you are trying to drain. This all sounds utterly self-evident, yet I have been asked many times why shrubs on one side of a drive do well while on the other side they perish. Too often the drive is cutting off drainage and making the unhappy shrubs stand in water most of the time. This is also the reason for numerous fatalities among foundation plantings—water pours off the roof and is then trapped around the roots of the plants when it cannot drain around the impermeable foundation. Go back and read over all the information on drainage that you skipped when you first started to garden. Drainage is a vital part of winter survival, and you may be only starting to realize it. Better drainage can often increase the range of plants we can grow by an entire climate zone.

For some plants, ordinary drainage is not enough. A further step in the water wars is creating a scree. A natural scree is the accumulation of broken rock and plant debris that forms at the base of a mountain slope. A garden scree is a deep bed filled mostly with rocks, then topped with a mixture of

topsoil, gravel, and sand. This may seem like the kind of extreme action only resorted to by eccentric rock gardeners, but your plants may convince you otherwise. Many of my more demanding specimens made a rapid migration out of the perennial beds and took root with much greater success in a scree area I had originally prepared for alpines. Dainty dianthus were soon crowded out by towering verbascums, whose felty rosettes turn to mush in greener pastures. This was bad enough, but at least the plants were still in the garden. When the hollyhocks trooped out of their border into the gravel driveway, I started to get the message about drainage and began parking the car on the front lawn. Water gathering at the crowns of some perennials results in rot. Soil that is mostly gravel, or a gravel mulch over the surface of a bed, keeps crowns and lower leaves dry and discourages the fungi and bacteria that cause rot. Beds of gravel may sound strange, but you will find that many plants grow well in that situation.

The English, not surprisingly, have long recognized the problems of excess moisture, even in their much milder climate, and have developed their own eccentric ways of dealing with it—one of which is the cloche. This is a glass bell that is placed over specimens to keep them dry. Modern technology has brought this item into the twentieth century by making plastic cloches, which at least alleviates the problems that occur when your large dog chases a rabbit through your cloche-dotted border. Arranging plastic cones in our landscape might seem to be the limit of absurdity, but these handy little hats can protect choice seedlings or delicate transplants from rabbits and mice; they can prevent frost damage to susceptible species in early spring; and they may be just what you need for that one plant you are longing to grow.

Not all of the aspects of climate we have discussed will be problematic in your garden. Not all of the modifications suggested will work for you. But perhaps you have begun to appreciate our many climates and to understand what you can do to garden in them successfully. Sometimes just one change can make it possible for you to grow ten or twenty new plants. And one of them might be the flower that brings the border to life in August, or the tree whose foliage is such a treat in mid-December, or the bulb you needed to bring an extra week of spring. These are the plants that can make any effort seem worthwhile.

Catastrophes

GARDENING IS NOT easy in North America. New gardeners consistently underrate the challenges involved, especially if they have immersed themselves in British garden literature. After ten years we may be only beginning to understand our particular climate and how it affects every aspect of life out-of-doors. But beside the aspects of climate that we can anticipate, there are the periodic catastrophes that no amount of understanding can prevent. This past year, for instance, was a particularly violent one, and many gardens in the region will take years to recover. We had a storm of terrible force in early winter, followed by a new year of almost unmatched cold and snow, capped by a blizzard, which, although not the blizzard of the century, was a significant event for most of us. This was just in the East. In the West, after several years of drought and fire, Southern California had its second winter of drenching rains, resulting in fatal mudslides and flooding. In the

Midwest, an enormous swath of America's richest farmland, as well as countless homes, were under many feet of floodwater for weeks.

But the above catalog, with a few variations, could be written about almost any American garden year. In England they are still bemoaning the storm of October 1987, which devastated many fine gardens and destroyed invaluable trees. But in the years since that storm, America has suffered many of similar magnitude and a few of greater strength. Storms which, at their height, seemed like once-in-a-lifetime experiences become blurred in memory by more recent disasters—who now remembers in what year two feet of snow covered the Northeast the first week in October, or when an ice storm in March sawed off thousands of trees and plunged Rochester, New York, into darkness for ten days? Only months ago Hurricane Andrew was fresh in our minds, but how many will recall it by the time they read this book? Who can remember the name of the 1990 hurricane that put Charleston, South Carolina, underwater and dismembered gardens that had bloomed for a century?

It is impossible not to feel some degree of despair as we survey the damage: huge old trees pulled up by the roots and flung on top of others; shrubs literally flattened by the weight of ice and snow or battered by debris and rising floodwater. Our gardens and our landscapes are shaped constantly by this kind of disaster. It is never easy to face such damage, but catastrophes of climate inevitably are part of the context of gardening in America. In a way, such acts of God are easier to face than some aspects of the midlife crisis, since we don't have to feel personally responsible. Quiet resignation seems the most reasonable response. We can't garden in a climate of fear, waiting for the next branch to fall. We should avoid relying on a few spectacular specimens or on a certain flowering effect, since we never know when these might fail us. A garden is not made memorable by only one tree, or even by ten; a landscape is composed of many elements, some rising, some in decline. When a favorite tree falls, we will mourn its passing; but now there is light where there was once shade, and some plants that once struggled will now begin to thrive. In the blackened landscape of a forest fire springs up a wilderness of wildflowers. Extremes are part of our lives on this continent; they must be part of any garden we create.

10

Onward and

Outward

in the Garden

....

Where DO WE go from here? The garden will continue to grow and change over time. Our intervention will determine how much of it survives and what direction it takes in the future, but some of our plant material is probably prepared to go on without us if necessary, and some of it has plans for the future we may not anticipate. We will probably never again face the kind of crisis we encountered at the end of our first gardening decade, but that doesn't mean that we have taken control once and for all. The changes will be slower, and if we have learned from our experiences, we will be more prepared to deal with them as they arise. However, there will always be too much and too many of some things, and too little of others, something we eventually discover in all areas of life.

What I want to suggest in this farewell chapter are some of the ways the garden may grow in the next decade and beyond. We can anticipate changes and prepare for them, we can even try to prevent them, but the aging process is as inevitable for an oak as it is for each one of us. We will probably find that the aging of our gardens is somewhat more enjoyable to observe than our personal maturation; in fact, the former can be a distraction from and a solace for the latter. But before turning to the changes of the garden over time, I would like to suggest some of the ways the garden may expand in space during its next decade.

Now that you have survived this first predictable crisis, you might very well be looking for new worlds to conquer. This does not necessarily entail the physical expansion of the garden. Some of you will pursue more and more difficult and out-of-the-way plants. This could occupy you happily for the rest of your days, and there are scores of books that can guide you in your search for the iris species of China, or the bulbs of the mountains of what used to be Czechoslovakia. But some of you, particularly if you own more than an acre or two, may want to explore the possibilities of the larger landscape.

As we observed earlier, most of us start to garden in the immediate surroundings of our houses. Gradually, through the first decade, we expand; how far we go depends on the limits of the property and the limits of our energy and resources. During the first ten years we begin to determine the kinds of plants we like to grow, the kinds of plants we can grow, what it takes to grow them, and how much space they need. One thing we may not have given much thought to is how the cultivated areas of our property relate to the spaces around them.

In a small lot, the question of relating the garden to the space around it will eventually become moot—sooner or later the garden will simply fill all available space. This is part of the charm of the cottage garden, where every inch is filled with flowers. But that kind of a garden works only in a compact space. A wall or fence or hedge can be used to section off part of a larger property, creating the sense of compression offered by a cottage plot—spaces that some call "garden rooms." But unless there are natural boundaries to follow, or unless the transition from enclosed to unclosed is managed very skillfully, the isolated area can end up either feeling like a claustrophobic extension of the house or looking like a flowery island floating in a sea of suburban lawn. It is thrilling to be the proud possessor of an acre or three or five, but just what is one to do with all that ground? The familiar suburban answer for the last fifty years has been lawn and trees and shrubs. Those are the elements you have been using, no doubt, but you might consider ways of enhancing their effect.

Many of us have been prone to binges of specimen planting throughout our gardening lives and we know how it works: you read about all the wonderful trees in the world; you visit a botanical garden; you visit a well stocked nursery; and suddenly you find you have scattered sixteen or thirty different species, one of each, willy-nilly around the landscape. Practically speaking, there are few surer ways to define the limits of your climate zone than by killing off a few ill-chosen woody plants. But even after clearing out the early fatalities this random selection dotted about usually does not result in a coherent garden picture. As these specimens mature and as we continue to plant more of them, the grounds come to resemble a crazy quilt more than a garden.

Trees are a wonderful way to use the outer edges of a property, since after the first year or two they will require relatively little attention. You can find trees that will utilize the poor soil and difficult exposure in those areas of the yard where you thought nothing would grow. But as long as you keep sticking them around one by one, ten yards apart, they are going to look like a nursery closeout sale. You will only see each plant as an individual unit, not as part of a larger pattern.

In nature, trees tend to grow in clusters. You may see an isolated ancient oak or magnificent ash that has outlasted everything around it, and some trees like the black walnut release growth inhibitors that shut down any nearby competition. But most trees are gregarious; they have growth patterns that encourage clumps of the same species. Locust trees and sassafras produce abundant root suckers; when you begin to look around, particularly in winter when tree forms are more clearly apparent, you will notice that you rarely see one of those trees alone. Birch and aspen similarly group themselves, and the beauty of those gold or silver groves far surpasses the effect a single tree can achieve. Broken branches of willow sprout and root easily in water, building up heavy-headed clusters along ponds and streams. Your yard need not be a slavish imitation of nature, but some trees simply look better in groups. Small-scale understory trees, such as redbud or shadblow, are lovely single specimens for a little garden, but in a larger landscape their fragile charms can be lost unless they are used en masse. A single pine or spruce can be monumental, but a group of evergreens makes a mysterious and inviting cavern in the midst of otherwise featureless space.

All this is an argument for reorganizing some of your tree plantings. Think of making groves where once there were single specimens. This offers several advantages for your garden as a whole. Once you abolish the pattern of lawn-and-specimen-tree planting, you will find that you can use more plants. And you can use land that you have no interest in including in the more inhabited parts of the garden, like the front yard. (How many suburban front yards are social and horticultural wastelands, visited weekly by the lawn mower, but no one else?) You can break up monotonous expanses of space, separating them into more intriguing configurations of sun and shade. A partially seen, sunlit clearing has more appeal than the familiar spread of grass, absorbed in one glance. Clusters of different sizes, shapes, and textures, with broken areas of lawn in between, are an attractive way to close out unattractive views of neighbors or streets—preferable to fences or a rigid hedge of one kind of plant. And just think—you will have less and less lawn to water, weed, and mow. Gradually the grass will thin out and slow down as the trees mature. You can let it grow much longer between the trees—that will give the effect of open parkland, a welcome departure from the blank inevitability of lawn.

Will it look silly to start planting smaller, younger trees around a specimen that has a ten-year head start? This is often how groves develop in nature: a single tree matures and begins seeding offspring or throwing up root suckers in the vicinity. The difference in size will be noticeable for the first few years, negligible after that.

Each grove need not consist of only a single species, but consider carefully whether different trees have compatible habits of growth before you group them. Clumps of birch silhouetted against dark conifers make a lovely picture, but if you don't gauge your spacing those delicate birch will end up within the spruces instead of outside them.

Groves of trees are not just an attractive feature in themselves. They can become areas for further planting, depending on your ambitions. Deciduous trees provide ideal sites for bulbs like narcissus or endymion; primroses, epimedium, day lilies, and digitalis will all bloom happily in light shade, depending on the severity of your climate and your deer problem. There are lots of understory shrubs you could plant once the trees are tall enough to accommodate them. If you already have a lot of plants in cultivation you won't want these wooded isles to get too demanding, but they offer possibilities for expansion if you feel the urge someday. Small sections of open ground between the groves are good places to experiment with meadow flowers; often it is difficult to make a graceful transition from manicured grass to naturalized plantings, and an isolated clearing surrounded by trees is a delightful place to discover an outburst of wildflowers.

The size of your property will dictate the number and size of your groves and the kind of trees you use. Even a small yard can benefit from a group of the slender silverbells, *Halesia carolina* or *Halesia monticola,* or a cluster of ginkgo, or some of the conifers with an upright habit. The dramatic taxodium, although not evergreen, is a spire-shaped conifer found naturally in groves on swampy ground.

Some trees are not candidates for this kind of planting—any specimen of a bizarre foliage type or a peculiar habit of growth, any species so exotic that it demands its own spotlight. These are trees for the more cultivated parts of the property, close to the house or pool or flower borders. Try to create the sense that you are moving from the garden out into nature. Flower borders and herb and vegetable beds are artificial entities, places where nature is controlled, contained. Topiary, variegated leaves, and weeping habit imply the efforts of man and should find a place within the domain of cultivation. A lawn with isolated specimen trees extends the manmade universe to the edge of your property lines. This may be what you want, but it greatly limits the range of expression of your property. Even half an acre is a lot of space for a highly cultivated garden. Anything more than that gives you ample room to provide a transition from cultivation to exploration, from the artificial to the almost natural. Even if what lies beyond your acre are the sidewalks and street signs of suburban life, you can create the impression of a more natural world around you by your selection of trees and the patterns of planting you employ.

A Final Word on Shade

THE ABOVE SCENARIO implies that your property is open and bright around the house, where you have established the flower borders, and moves out toward informal clusters of shrubs and groves of trees. But it might be the case that large old trees shade most of the area surrounding the house, with the only spots of sun shining on the driveway or at some inconvenient distance. You may have been gardening successfully for the last decade with only a few hours of direct sun, and if you have, my hat is off to you. There are, of course, wonderful plants for shade. There are wonderful gardens made in shade. Most visitors to the Connecticut garden of the late Lincoln Foster became convinced that the best condition for a garden is light shade. But for those of us who are not such brilliant gardeners, unrelieved shade

is not an asset. It is desirable if you don't have much of it, but if it is all you have, your gardening life is a challenge. I think that if I had been gardening for ten years in shade the next stage in the garden would be to see what trees I could live without.

One feature of shade is that, barring intervention from hurricanes and ice storms, there is more of it every year. You must be constantly on the alert in the next decade to see that the creeping shadows don't engulf parts of the garden where they are not wanted. It is pleasant to have a few large shade trees near the house, but they don't have to be on top of it, they don't have to surround it, and they don't have to carpet every inch with darkness. That is the situation with many homes in older suburbs. All of us in the garden business have been asked over and over, "What will do well in three hours of sun?" Well, there are answers to that, and I am sure in ten years of gardening you have come across some of them. But too many people use their lack of light as an excuse for all their failures, instead of finding ways to let the sun shine in. Full sun is necessary for a large number of plants, and it will make the cultivation of many borderline shade plants a great deal easier. If you feel you have reached a dead end in the dark, don't wait to see a light at the end of the tunnel. It might be a long time before the next hurricane. Grit your teeth and make your own light—take down a few trees.

More Distant Horizons

W H A T I F Y O U have more than an acre or three—what if you have twenty, or fifty, or two hundred? This is not at all unlikely in many parts of America, especially as farms have died out and country homes have taken their places. The changeover has been unfortunate but inevitable, and many country-home buyers have found it cheaper to buy fifty acres than five.

"We just bought a hundred acres; what should we do with it?" This was the garden question I heard over and over throughout the seventies when the country-home land rush began in earnest. The most reasonable answer is, "Do nothing." For the first ten years, fix up the house, start a garden on one acre, and let the rest continue to do what it has been doing for the last few decades. As you slowly get to know your property, your climate, your own interests and capabilities, you can begin to think of modifying some of those acres.

Whether you have five acres or a hundred, what you probably want from your land is the greatest diversity that can be managed in that space. If you have only woods, you might want to start clearing meadows. If your property has been open farmland, it will quickly start evolving into something else unless you do something about it. Trees and brush will move in as the acreage proceeds away from grassland toward woody climax forest. If you have no woods, you will probably want to let some acres move in that direction; you may want to plant trees to hasten your woods along.

If you want to maintain open fields of grass, you must have them mowed at least once a year. Perhaps there are local farmers who want the hay and will cut it for you; otherwise you should cut it at the end of the summer and let the grass molder back into the soil. If you let the mowing lapse for several years until brush has a foothold, or if you are trying to reclaim old meadows, you will need to employ a brush hog (called a bush hog in some places), a mower adapted for moving over rough ground and cutting woody plants. The transition stages between meadow and forest are fascinating to observe; they will offer you great diversity of plant and animal life. But the charms of a meadow are equally compelling, so if mowing is available you may want to keep some areas in that state. A meadow will still need mowed paths during the times between cutting. Besides making the meadow accessible, such paths can be important visual elements, drawing the eye and the imagination past the cultivated foreground out into the world of possibilities.

What is the difference between a meadow and a pasture? A pasture, by definition, has animals grazing on it, which shapes the land in yet another way. A pasture has a short grass surface for most of the summer. If cows are grazing, they will eliminate almost everything except big thistles and clumps of *Iris missouriensis* in the damp places. Horses are much more erratic grazers, leaving sweeps of buttercups and daisies and areas of long grass scattered about. If some of your land is fenced, you might ask if any of your neighbors want to use it for grazing. (Portable electric fencing has made it easy and inexpensive to set up short-term pastures, even in places that have been open land.) This may seem an eccentric suggestion, but there are several ways grazing can benefit your property overall. A short-cropped surface is very pleasant for walking—a nice change from the tall grass of a meadow. Grazing will eliminate the need for mowing, and there is the ever-changing beauty provided by animals moving across the landscape. These may not be sufficient reasons to subsidize a herd of cows yourself, but if someone else can use the land in this way you may find it delightful. My husband has never had the least interest in our horses, but he loves the way they look out in the field beyond the garden. A grazing pasture need not be land lost to planting, but if you plant young trees you will need to protect them for several years.

There are some drawbacks to having pastures and meadows within reach of your garden. One is that the picturesque cows and horses are always convinced that the grass is greener on your manicured lawns. Good fences definitely make good neighbors, but even the best fences occasionally give in to pressure. These brief invasions, however, are nothing compared to the constant traffic of more persistent pests. One of the joys of a large country garden is the chance to look out across those rolling acres of grass and wildflowers. One of the headaches is the parade of grasses and wildflowers into your beds and borders. Try to maintain a broad swath of mowed area between your garden and the wild. High grass also provides cover for the many animals you may want to keep at a distance. An open, mowed no-man's-land will help, but wildlife is something you will have to be prepared for.

Into the Woods

WHAT IF YOUR surrounding acres are forest? Large stands of mature trees are so beautiful in themselves that little has to be done to improve upon them. Your main concern is making your woods accessible—we are back to the importance of paths. Spend a lot of time figuring out where you want to go and how quickly you want to get there. Mark out routes and try them over and over before you make them permanent paths. Is there a natural goal for your woodland walk—an abandoned quarry, a stream or spring, a spectacular view? You may want to have some routes that move directly toward their target, others that circle in a leisurely fashion. There could be a woodland walk to a place where trillium grow, another that seeks out chanterelles. Discover what natural treasures your woods conceal, then find pleasant ways to get there. This may be a very slow-moving project—it may be years before you move away from your garden to explore the wilderness. But once you start exploring, your woods could become another part of the extended garden.

After you have established the routes you want to take, set to work making permanent, comfortable paths. Remember the lessons taught by your earlier garden paths—make them broad, solid, and not too steep. You may have been content scrambling up deer tracks during your early explorations, but that will be less and less appealing as time wears on and never inviting to friends out for a stroll. As with meadow paths, the visual impact of a woodland path is as important as its practical advantages. A mass of woodland is often too overwhelming for us to take in all at once; even if it is possible to walk through it, we may feel that we can hardly see it. A road or path shapes the masses into distinguishable parts; it provides a necessary axis around which the natural beauty can be organized in ways with which we are familiar. The path connects the wild to the civilized; it implies the presence of man, something your less adventurous visitors will find reassuring. A path need not intrude on the life of the forest, and it makes it possible for us to share it.

The property of two friends in my neighborhood comes vividly to mind as I think about woodland paths. Louise Fishman and Betsy Crowell bought an old house and twenty-five acres about six years ago. Their property was the familiar combination offered by abandoned farmland—open meadows near the house, a small, steep woodland stream, and broad stretches of mature oak-maple-beech forest. A path wanders through the meadow to a small screened teahouse by the stream. From there, broad walks circle through the woods, turning and crossing smaller tracks so that you are never quite sure how far you have come or if you have been here before. The paths eventually come out on an isolated field with a small pond.

The shaping of the landscape began when Louise and Betsy made the pond and connected it to the house by a direct route. But once they found a bulldozer operator they could trust, the possibilities of further paths became alluring. Louise says, "I just walked and walked, especially in winter, and in summer I scrambled through the brush. A man from the DEC advised me on which trees to cut, so that made some of the decisions. I went around with surveyor's tape and marked the paths and kept trying them until they seemed to work." A small bulldozer took the job from there. Two years later, when I first saw them, the paths had the look and feel of roads that had been part of the woods for a century. The paths made by Louise and Betsy make their fifteen acres of woods seem almost limitless. A much larger woods, like my own, gives less pleasure because it is not as well organized and is more difficult to experience.

The woods you have may not be the woods you want. They could be crowded with saplings and underbrush, a woods-on-the-way instead of the forest primeval. Time will remedy some of that, but you could help things along by thinning and clearing. Your local conservation agency can give you

advice on which trees to encourage, which trees to dispose of. This kind of scrubby woods can be particularly unpleasant unless you have a path, so, once again, that is the first priority.

It may seem perverse to recommend planting trees in some places and cutting them down in others, but I believe that a property of any size benefits from the alternation between light and shade, between closed and open. Our land includes a wooded hill of about 140 acres, some of it mature trees, some very steep scrub, some old pasture thickly grown with saplings. Three years ago we decided to clear one of those old fields to open up a spectacular view and to provide variety from the rest of the woodland. I really had no idea how enjoyable a project this would be or in how many ways it would benefit the landscape. We decided not to make the meadow completely open, so we marked certain trees to be saved—strong young oaks, a cluster of birch, clumps of white pine, and some sugar maples. The first summer the seven-acre space looked rather raw and patchy—brambles sprang up, there were blackened areas where brush had been burned, suckers tried to grow from the old trunks. All that was cured by a brush hog last fall. This summer we have a meadow that could compete with any wildflower calendar—snowy drifts of daisies, tall spires of verbascum, wild thyme, and strawberries underfoot. The field has become a natural destination of walks through the woods, so a series of paths has been established. (It has also become the destination of wildlife; we have been unable to get rid of the last brush piles, because the turkeys have nested there each season.) What was once a non-descript and impassable growth of trees has become a bright new part of the landscape. And we have enough firewood to last a lifetime.

Scale is an important consideration in shaping a larger landscape, just as it is crucial in shaping more cultivated areas. In a woods of one hundred acres, a meadow of one acre would have almost no impact. On a five-acre property, two or three acres of woods can seem like a forest, and a quarter-acre meadow will have the effect of a much greater expanse.

Water Works

IT IS PROBABLY unnecessary to say that I am a great believer in ponds. Who wouldn't be? What single element can so transform a landscape as water can? The size, shape, depth, and character—deep and tranquil, or shallow and bustling with life—are dependent on the landscape, the soil, and your budget, but in any area other than the drylands of America a pond is an irresistible possibility. I look from my office out across the ever-changing surface of our first pond and I know I never could have made a garden without it, without its cooling depths, without the quiet contrast it provides to the vitality of the flowers. Not that it is so quiet when you look closely —this morning I have seen the muskrats swimming with their loads, back and forth a dozen times. I can see the painted turtles sunning on the far bank; the green heron stalks the grassy rim. This may be entirely too much life for some gardeners, but this is a country garden—there are less energetic ponds and pools available for other landscapes. The technology of plastic pond liners has improved so greatly in recent years that a small pond can be installed on even the most porous soil.

The making of a pond is a somewhat more complicated business today than it once was. Environmental regulations might seem like a nuisance, but they are desirable precautions for the wetlands of our country as a whole. The Department of Environmental Conservation in your area may have to determine if your potential pond interrupts any important drainage systems and make sure that it conforms to certain safety regulations. These strictures vary from one area to the next—your cooperative extension agency can probably tell you all you need to know, as well as provide you with names of local contractors. In most cases the DEC encourages ponds (especially those of moderate size), because they benefit wildlife. A year after our most recent pond was built, a DEC representative called to ask if we had noticed any new birds or animals in the area. This solicitude can occasionally work against you. Wetland regulations have been strengthened so that once you have a permanent body of water you can't lightly dispose of it. And if you have a small pond that you wish to enlarge, you may have to convince the regulators that you are improving the wetland, not reducing it. When you consider how many thousands of acres of irreplaceable wetland have been lost to development in this country, you will appreciate the importance of regulation, even if it causes unexpected paperwork.

Ponds, pastures, woods, meadows—one of the pleasures of the extended garden is that these natural elements have so much to offer at times when the cultivated garden is inactive. The autumn woods are just coming alive with color when the flower beds are blackening with frost. A brisk walk across open fields in February is a welcome alternative to peering at the stony ground and wondering if anything has survived the winter. A pond is alive with early salamanders and spring peepers long before the first daffodils appear.

The goal of the legendary English landscape designers of the eighteenth century was to form the land into a series of idealized natural pictures, with rolling pastures, curving streams, dramatic views, inviting woodlands. Walking or driving through different parts of America, I have realized that many of us have more nature at our disposal than Humphry Repton ever dreamed of. You don't have to be a duke to put in a pond or open up a vista; it doesn't take the wealth of generations to clear a field. A garden can be much more than a series of flower beds clustered around the back door. Move out into your landscape and discover how much it can bring back into the garden.

As Time Goes By

M A N Y   A S P E C T S   O F gardening become easier after the first ten years. You may not have conquered every weed in your neighborhood, but at least you can recognize the most invasive of them and act promptly. You may not have experienced every insect or illness known to ornamental plants, but you have probably endured the most likely afflictions, developing your personal regimen against the worst and inuring yourself to the rest. After ten years your plants are big enough to shrug off the pests that had you hysterical in the early days.

Big plants are easier in many ways, once you recognize their space needs and allow for them, which few of us do. We look at our borders in April or May and cannot imagine, even after years of success, that the humble mound of new delphinium leaves will eventually produce seven-foot spires —before it falls over. Many of us continue to have a pathological fear of gaps, even though by June there will hardly be space to insert a trowel in the borders, much less another plant.

Big plants and lots of them will enable you, finally, to create those great sweeps of color you read about so hungrily in the beginning, back when you wondered if a six-pack of impatiens could count as a sweep. If you have a preoccupation with color schemes, their realization is easier, too—now that you know when plants bloom for you, as opposed to when they bloom for Rosemary Verey. It takes many years of gardening to recognize how specific are the blooming periods for each individual garden and each plant. There are some commonplace combinations we are all bound to repeat, but as your garden matures you can seek out color effects that are unique to your plants and your taste.

On the other hand, you might find that you care less than you once did about fussy questions of color. Once you have masses of flowers in bloom, many of the obsessive preoccupations of the early days seem not to matter. You may become accustomed to the startling way nature puts colors together—can any of us match the boldness of the orange of the fruit of the *Euonymus alatus* paired with its fuchsia interior? There will always be some gardeners who have a better eye for color than the rest of us, and who combine flowers brilliantly. There will be some who continue to employ color schemes as self-effacing as those of a corporate office interior. And there will be many who decide, when faced with an exuberant display in brilliant sunshine, that they really don't care that the tiger lilies look a little weird with the hollyhocks.

Keeping Your Garden Alive

WHEN PERENNIALS ARE large and settled, it is easier to keep track of them—they don't meet the fate of slender seedlings that get lost in the spring shuffle. But you will, I hope, continue to experiment with plants whose cultural requirements are either peculiar or unknown, even though you might occasionally have to suffer the consequences.

Keep an eye on your larger woody plants in the years to come. In ten years, your perennials have gone about as far as they can go in terms of size, except for those invasive root-running species. At least you have a fair notion of the dimensions of your more enduring herbaceous plants and can plan accordingly. But many of your shrubs will not have reached maturity in a decade, and your trees are barely beginning to get off the ground.

I have already cautioned you about the dangers of encroaching shade; don't think that you have fought the last battle on that front. As long as your trees continue to grow, you will have to keep adjusting your plantings accordingly, and they will continue to grow for decades after you have ceased to garden. Mature trees and shrubs are among the joys of the older garden, but you have to be prepared for them. The changes may be slow and barely perceptible, lulling you into a false sense of security. Then suddenly you will find yourself fighting your way through the garden again, just as you did after its first decade.

There are more subtle ways a garden can lose vitality in the coming years. You can simply get into a rut. You can become bored with the same plant combinations and indifferent to the familiar cycles of bloom. We will never exhaust the possibilities of the plant world, but at times we may need encouragement to seek them out. The best remedy for horticultural ennui, and any number of other garden ills, is visiting.

You can never see too many gardens. (You can see too many in one day, but that is usually the fault of tour organizers.) Americans are only beginning to realize this, and unfortunately much of their garden touring has been directed to gardens abroad. The great gardens of other cultures and other climates can always inspire and teach us, but we could all benefit from seeing gardens closer to home. And not just great gardens. Find out what is going on in your neighborhood. You don't have to wait for a tour—just get on the phone. For several years, five or six of us in this area spent a day going around to each other's gardens. It was interesting to see how different each garden was from the others, even though we share the same climate, soil, and landscape. There were plants we all used, but in various ways, and in each setting they performed and looked different. And each garden had plants that were unique to it, which suggested new possibilities.

If you are not inclined to go bursting into gardens on your own, there are tours offered by garden clubs and horticultural organizations. It seems as if more and more charity groups are using garden parties and tours for fund-raising. Get on some mailing lists and find out what is out there.

The Garden Conservancy is a new organization in America dedicated to rehabilitating and preserving historic gardens and keeping them open to the public. American gardeners are only beginning to be aware of their garden heritage, and the Conservancy is making it possible for us to preserve and witness it.

Visiting old gardens is the best way to prepare for the changes we may experience in our gardens in years to come. It is impossible for most of us to imagine what our trees and shrubs are going to look like in maturity. More important, it is impossible to understand how the changing scale of our framework plants will influence our design and our plantings in the future. Old gardens can be a revelation in this way. You may be adjusting to the size and shape of an Alberta spruce ten or fifteen years old—wait until you see what one looks like when it's forty. Plants we may have thought of as reliable after a decade's acquaintance begin to exhibit unexpected vices as they age—thinning out at the bottom, breaking off at the top. In an old formal garden I saw recently I was struck by what appeared to be two evergreen umbrellas sticking up on either side of a stairway, interrupting a glorious view. Was it possible that such ludicrous topiary was intentional? Old photographs reveal that the two parasols were originally knee-high mounds. Over the decades they had pushed upward on naked trunks until they achieved today's comic effect—one the original designer could never have imagined. Such visions remind us that gardens are always growing, always changing. There will never be an end to digging up, cutting back, moving out. These are among the labors of the garden, but they contribute to its inexhaustible beauty through time.

Time is a partner in our garden making in the years ahead. We do not know all the changes it has to contribute; we cannot imagine some of the revelations yet to come. Many plants have very different characters as they age, and the spaces they inhabit will change with them. Much of our gardening in the future will depend on recognizing these changes and making the most of them. A garden is a mixture of the ephemeral and the enduring. We must work to keep the balance between the moments of fleeting beauty and the solid strength of generations. The more long-lived plants may begin to overawe the garden; it is up to us to keep the plantings from becoming static. There should always be something to look forward to.

I am on the threshold of beginning an old garden, of moving into a garden that was made and loved long before I was born. I feel as if I have never understood the majesty of old plants and how they influence everything around them. Most of all I feel how forcefully a garden expresses the person who makes it. After ten years our gardens are only beginning to show our opinions, our habits, our points of view. In the years to come, all these become more apparent as the garden grows in personality until it becomes a unique expression of ourselves. There are those who insist that a garden is too transitory to claim the status of art. Yet I walk in this garden that has been empty for years and I feel, vibrantly, the life of the woman who made it. Let us hope that all our gardens may someday have such power.

Index

··

eupatorium, 80
evergreens, 4, 5, 6, 27, 45, 56, 72, 168, 185
   see also conifers

false Solomon's seal, 78
ferns, 99
Fishman, Louise, 192
flax (linum), 59, 112
flowering almond (prunus), 53
flowering quince (chaenomeles), 166
forget-me-not, 65
forsythia, 33, 166, 167
Foster, Lincoln, 187
foundation planting, 6, 26
fritillaria, 38, 55
   Fritillaria meleagris, 38
fritillary butterfly, 128

gaillardia, 60
Garden Conservancy, 19, 198
gentian, 17
geranium, 117
germander, 99
ginkgo, 186
Giverney, 14
gladiolus, 113–14
   Gladiolus byzantinus, 114
   G. x colvillei, 114
globe arborvitae, 30
godetia, 113
Golden Age, 7, 9, 14, 15
golden glow (*Rudbeckia laciniata*), 35
goldenrod (solidago), 59, 131
gray-brown Podzolic soil, 144
Great Dixter, 106
Greene, Isabelle, 140
ground covers, 11, 23, 65, 85, 94, 139
gypsophila, 117

Halesia carolina, 186–87
Halesia monticola, 186–87
Hamamelis virginiana (witch hazel), 71
heliotrope, 113
hellebore, 68–69
   Helleborus niger (Christmas rose), 68–69
   H. orientalis (Lenten rose), 68–69

herbaceous plants, 35, 36, 45, 53, 60, 103, 104,
   145, 166, 169, 174
   see also perennials
herbs, 7, 10, 12, 19, 30, 92, 99
hesperis, 39, 76, 156
Hidcote, 103, 106
hollyhock, 129, 177, 197
homeria, 114
honeybee, 123, 128
honeysuckle (lonicera), 33, 71
hydroxyl ions, 114, 149, 159
hymenoptera, 128

Ilex verticillata, 71–72, 171
impatiens, 7, 111, 171
ipheion, 38
iris, 17, 35, 37, 39, 69, 80, 93, 108, 117, 183
   Iris histrioides, 69
   I. missouriensis, 190
   I. pseudacorus, 39
   I. reticulata, 69
   Japanese, 108
   Siberian, 39, 93, 108, 117
ixia, 114

jack-in-the-pulpit (arisaema), 99
Jekyll, Gertrude, 103, 105, 109, 110
juniper, 10, 26, 30–31, 72, 92
   Juniperus chinensis "Pyramidalis", 30–31

kudzu, 4, 138

laburnum, 7
lamiastrum, 66
larch (larix), 72–73
lawn, 6, 9, 10, 13, 23, 38, 60, 77, 85, 87, 88, 97, 98,
   104, 131, 132, 133, 184–87
leaf miner, 50
lewisia, 88
liatris, 109, 131
life cycles, 4, 52–55
ligularia, 109
lilac, 24, 29, 33, 170
lily of the valley, 66
linden (tilia), 74, 129
Lloyd, Christopher, 106